KUDOS FOR THE 1ST EDITION

"You're in the feed store, peering quizzically at the label on a 50-pound sack, when a fellow shopper comes over to help. Turns out he's a rancher who spent seven years as president and CEO of a nutritional supplement company. In about 15 minutes, he's walked you through the nutrients on the label, describing what they mean for your horse's stage of life and level of activity, and suddenly the mystery of feeding seems perfectly clear. That's how you'll feel when you read *Beyond the Hay Days*....this pleasant little primer contains an impressive amount of science and a healthy dose of common sense from a man who's been raising and feeding horses successfully for years."

— EQUUS

"If you'd like to get a handle on equine nutrition, but the subject tends to make your eyes glaze over, add *Beyond the Hay Days* to your horse library...Ewing will answer most, if not all of your questions. And don't overlook the book's tiny Appendix, which will enable you to customize your horse's ration....Ewing delivers what he promises on the cover— a refreshingly simple guide to effective horse nutrition."

— Horse & Rider

"This fascinating and folksy book takes a very dry subject and makes it interesting....Ewing discusses the needs of different horses, such as why the energetic stallion consumes more energy than mares and geldings, and gives some general management tips that will be useful to anyone. Some of this information is hard to find, such as what MSM is and what it seems to do. Ewing wraps it up... using the KISS principle (keep it simple, stupid). For those of us not seeking a doctorate in equine nutrition, this book pretty well covers what we need to know."

— The Quarter Horse Journal

".... He [Ewing] is a horseman who appreciates the art of feeding as much, if not more so, than the science of it. But he also fully appreciates the words nutritionists use with ease: macrominerals, fat-soluble and water-soluble vitamins, chondroitin sulfates, and more. The difference in Ewing's approach is that he translates the big words and percentages found on most feed and supplement labels into a more easily understood frame of reference."

— Western Horseman

"The author has taken a complicated subject and made it not only understandable but also interesting, so what I thought was going to be a slog through a ton of nutritional facts turned out to be a breeze to read.... The formulas are based on weight and performance needs, making this book useful for owners of all breeds including drafts."

— Rural Heritage

continued

"This thin, easy-to-read book uses common sense as its guiding force and knits in those complicated equations so the reader learns—and enjoys while doing so. Author Rex Ewing writes this book like a long magazine article—and I mean a good magazine article. It's lively, full of fun and gets the information to the reader in a hurry...I highly recommend this book as an inexpensive, reliable and easy-to-swallow guide for experienced and green horsemen....For those of us who hate science and complicated dissertations, this is the book of choice."

— National Sporting Library

"Ewing is an excellent writer who consistently makes the information he conveys interesting and wellworth wading through. We learn, for instance, how to read a feed bag label—no small skill—and we get, along the way, a primer on converting to the metric system, favored by feed manufacturers....Ewing reminds us that "no two horses share the same biological makeup, or nutritional tolerances." Therefore, he doesn't dismiss that old standby, the horseman's eye....Beyond the Hay Days is a great reference as well as a delight to read."

— Horseplay

"It's about time! In an industry inundated with technical nutrition manuals, finally a nutritional guide for the everyday horseman that draws a clear mental image of usable equine nutrition. Thanks, Rex!"

— Joe Hatch, nutritionist & owner - Eqcel Horse Feed

"...a very concise and easy-to-read guide to feeding your horse. It gets the feed out of the bag and into your horse in the easiest terms."

— Lawrence R. Mackey, D.V.M.

"It's refreshing to find a treatise on the complicated subject of horse nutrition that explains many of the intricacies in a very understandable, educational yet entertaining manner. This is a must-read for all equine owners."

— Earl E. Ammerman, Ph.D.
Member of the American Feed Industry Association Nutrition Council

"Rex has taken the mystery out of how to calculate what a horse should have on a daily basis with excellent examples that we encounter in the day-to-day feeding of our horses."

— Jim Olson, nutritionist - Feed Products, Inc.

"For years people have asked me if there was a book that made horse nutrition less complicated than rocket science. Finally, I can say Yes!"

— Melanie Luark, nutritional adviser & horse owner

Beyond the Hay Days

Refreshingly Simple Horse Nutrition

UPDATED & EXPANDED 2ND EDITION

REX A. EWING

PIXYJACK PRESS LLC

—

Beyond the Hay Days: Refreshingly Simple Horse Nutrition

Published by PixyJack Press, LLC, PO Box 149, Masonville, CO 80541
www.pixyjackpress.com

9 8 7 6 5 4 3 2 1

First Edition 1997
Second Edition 2003

ISBN 0-9658098-4-6 paperback
ISBN 0-9658098-2-X hardcover

Library of Congress Cataloging-in-Publication Data
    Ewing, Rex A.
      Beyond the hay days : refreshingly simple horse nutrition / Rex A.
    Ewing.-- Updated & expanded 2nd ed.
        p. cm.
      ISBN 0-9658098-4-6 (pbk.) -- ISBN 0-9658098-2-X (hard cover)
    1. Horses--Feeding and feeds. 2. Horses--Nutrition. I. Title.
    SF285.5 .E97 2003
    636.1'085--dc211
                2003000757

Printed in the U.S.A. on ECF paper with soy ink.

Distributed to the trade by Johnson Books, Boulder, Colorado.
1-800-258-5830   www.johnsonbooks.com

Book design by LaVonne Ewing, Image Resource.
Illustrations by Sara Tuttle *(except pages 19, 27, 100, 123, 124, 143)*.

To LaVonne Ann,
who asked her cowboy to become a writer,
then gently nudged him away from his horses,
and his hayfield, long enough to become one.

CONTENTS

Part III: *The Extras and The Basics*

FOREWORD

Ahhhh.....that was a good read. Now when was the last time you said that as you finished a technical book?

One of the reasons I enjoy *Beyond the Hay Days* is because Rex Ewing is a cowboy poet trapped inside the pages of an equine nutrition book. Lucky us. What better combination for bringing a tough subject to life?

When you read about chelated minerals—you'll learn that the Latin "chelac" means "scorpion claws". Rex suggests that you imagine a scorpion holding a BB between the tips of its claws to get a picture of how the metal ion is held fast in a ring of electrons. Who else would tell you these things !?

I've long been a fan of combining art and science, no matter what the subject. Science can help make ethereal subjects materialize. And just the right touch of art can help demystify technical subjects, making them more accessible and even fun!

Our horses need to be fed properly. It's a big responsibility and just as with training, there is no one formula or plan for all horses. That's why it is essential to understand a certain amount of the science of nutrition so you can make your own intelligent, informed decisions.

If you've been looking for a down-to-earth equine nutrition reference, start reading and feeding.

CHERRY HILL

Cherry Hill is the author of 25 books on horse training and care. She and her husband, Richard Klimesh, are producing a series of equine videos and maintain an educational website at www.horsekeeping.com.

PROLOGUE

The horse is a spirit that lies so deeply buried within the human psyche that we often do not even realize it is there. And yet it is everywhere; there is no end to our fascination with these incredibly canny beasts. Even after 100 years of forsaking the horse for the horseless carriage (motorized transportation), the horse is still imbedded in our language. "Get back on the horse!" or "Quit horsing around!" are still common admonitions. On a summer day you might drive to a picnic in a vehicle rated in horsepower, eat sandwiches seasoned with horseradish sauce, then swat a few horseflies while playing a game of horseshoes. Look through any magazine—even one tailored to computer buffs—and you will see pictures of gracefully striding horses. Watch television on any given night and you will see ghostly images of the mythical, winged horse, Pegasus, morphing into a sporty new car.

Those of us who keep horses can only smile. We live a dream embraced by those who wish horses into their lives, only to find that they do not appear. Many people sell their homes in the city and, at no small expense, move to the country, just to be able to have a piece of that dream; a horse or two to ride and show. Others, like myself, have lived with horses for so long, a month in the tidal pools of New Guinea could not hide the fact from the nose of the common observer. We talk horses, we think horses, and we smell like horses. And we're proud of it.

I have always had horses in my life. I have been kicked and bitten, stomped on, bucked-off, and slammed into more fences than I care to recall. I have hobbled out of the house on crutches to ask the horse who put me in that condition if he was ready for the next round. I'm sure you know what I mean. If all of this abuse had been heaped upon me by the federal government, I would be looking for another country. But a horse is not a thing you can walk away from, or destroy. It is much too big for that; too big in sheer mass to manhandle, too big in spirit to deny.

From August of 1990 until April of this year, I was the president and CEO of a well-known company that derives nearly all of its revenues from the manufacture and sale of nutritional supplements for horses. It was not a job that I had dreamed of having, and I never felt that it suited my sensibilities, but it did set me on a seven-year mission to learn, as much as any simple horseman can, the best ways to help our horses through nutrition.

This book is the result of that 7-year search. In that time I have formulated a number of supplements that have been very successful in the marketplace, and equally successful for the horses in whose feed they ultimately ended up. But supplements are only the icing on the cake, not the cake itself. Most of the people who sought my advice over that time did not need supplements at all. They needed good, sound, basic nutrition; they needed to know what was inherently wrong with their feeding program, and how to correct it.

And that is my reason for writing this book. It was a fundamental decision, like drinking to slake a thirst, or eating to fill an empty belly. I had to write it because I owed it to the thousands of horse owners I have met and corresponded with over the years who needed a book such as this. People who, like all of us, wanted only the best for the beasts who are the keepers of our dreams.

Rex A. Ewing
July 1997

AUTHOR'S NOTE
TO THE 2ND EDITION

As I began gathering research for this updated and expanded second edition, I found myself marveling at how much had changed about horse nutrition in the few years since the appearance of the first edition. Glucosamine now overshadows chondroitin sulfates as the premiere ingredient in joint-maintenance formulations; new findings on the importance of magnesium—a heretofore pedestrian mineral—have recently surfaced; and, as in human nutrition, the Omega fatty acids have orbited into the spotlight.

But I was equally heartened to see how much had remained the same. The basic requirements for the energy nutrients—protein, fat, and carbohydrates—have not changed, nor have the requirements for most minerals. This is good. If it ain't broke, don't fix it, as we're all fond of saying. It means that after millennia of searching for better ways of feeding our noble steeds, we have finally discovered a solid, workable foundation to hang our faddish embellishments on.

This does not mean, however, that the end of horse nutrition is in sight. Far from it. As long as we have our horses, we will ask them to do things they would never do of their own accord, and feed them things they could never hope to find in their natural environment. Moreover, we will continue to breed for certain characteristics and against others. As we do, we will forever change the morphology of our horses, for selective breeding is still largely a guessing game, and unexpected changes always accompany the favorable traits we hope to infuse into the equine gene pool. Slightly different animals will always require subtly different concentrations of nutrients to remain in optimum condition.

This is good—and bad. Good because there are still countless advances waiting to be discovered in the world of nutrition (and no one satisfied with the status quo ever discovered anything), and bad because the market will forever have to endure the likes of hucksters and snake oil salesmen.

Hopefully, this updated and expanded edition will help you avoid the temptations so prevalent in a world where everyone is frantically searching for a panacea, and set you squarely on the path to solid horse nutrition.

Rex A. Ewing
January 2003

CHAPTER 1

The Art of Nutrition

1888

"Nature has evidently scattered variety, where the dull senses of man can perceive only sameness; and, to the temperate palate of the horse, the verdure of the fields may afford a delicious and an ever-varying banquet."

DR. EDWARD MAYHEW, *ILLUSTRATED HORSE MANAGEMENT*, 1888

While I was writing the first edition of this book, my wife and I lived in the Platte River valley on the eastern slope of Colorado. Just below our house we had about 15 acres of what is called sub-irrigated pasture. The water table is at, or just below, the surface. This land has never been farmed, and never will be. It is too wet for the plow; it's even too wet for most trees and broadleaf weeds. But it does produce an excellent variety of grass that stays vibrantly green from late April through mid-October, and will easily support fifteen horses during those months, even in a drought.

All of the minerals deposited there, through floods and other geologic forces over the millennia, are still there. The manure left by horses today is washed back into the soil to be taken up into the new-growth grass again tomorrow. I never had this grass analyzed, so from a scientific standpoint, I never really knew what was in it, and what wasn't. But from a practical standpoint, I knew that it would keep my horses healthy and happy for seven months of the year, as long as I dewormed them regularly, and provided them with water and salt. I also knew that if I gave my horses extra feed, they would have shinier coats, healthier feet, and brighter eyes. My foals would grow bigger and stronger, and their mothers would produce more milk.

When I feed supplements and sweet feed, I know exactly what I am giving to my horses, right down to the last milligram. Many would think it strange, or even remiss, that I would feed supplements without knowing the composition of the greater part of my horses' diets. How could I introduce such a large unknown into a controlled feeding program?

But what, exactly, was unknown? I knew that their grass provided nutrients within a range that is natural for the horse. If it didn't, I would have seen problems I never observed in horses on this pasture. I also knew that there is nothing toxic in the grass—it never caused lameness, gastric distress, abortions, abnormal growth, or unusual behavior. I knew, just like my father knew before I was born, that this particular 15 acres of ground provided almost everything a horse needs to live a long and healthy life, which is far more than I know about the things I feed myself!

There are hundreds of nutritionists who will analyze, to the last microgram, every nutrient in every speck of food a horse eats. I am not one of them. It is as pointless an endeavor as it is boring. The science of feeding horses is nothing like the science of building bridges. Every cable, every I-beam that comes out of a steel mill is built to a very narrow range of tolerances that can be plugged into an equation so the engineer will know what stresses the bridge will be able to endure. Not so with horses. Just as no two horses take to the bit in quite the same way, or feel exactly alike under saddle, no two horses share the same biological makeup, or nutritional tolerances. One horse will colic and die eating the same hay that another horse can eat day after day without so much as a mild belly-ache. An accidental grain ration sufficient to founder this horse will do nothing to that one.

Just as no two horses take to the bit in quite the same way, or feel exactly alike under saddle, no two horses share the same biological makeup, or nutritional tolerances.

And even if horses were as standardized as I-beams—a thoroughly depressing thought—the nutrients we give them are not. Fifty milligrams of copper looks the same on a guaranteed analysis, whether it is supplied by copper sulfate, or copper proteinate, or copper polysaccharide complex, but the number of copper ions making their way through the intestinal wall and into the bloodstream are quite different with each form of the mineral.

The issue at hand is as simple as it is profound: there is a point where the science of horse nutrition must graciously defer to the art of horse nutrition, and it is up to each horse owner to decide where that point is, with every horse he or she owns. My pasture of "unknown" content was, for me, the beginning of an art that began with the domestication of the horse. I could've had it analyzed for mineral content, protein and energy, but I would still not have known what was in my pasture. Each blade of grass is endowed with hundreds, if not thousands, of nutrients, each more subtle and elusive than the one before it. Unanalyzed, undissected—it remains a "whole," beyond quantification, beyond science.

By the time you finish reading this book, you will be able to read any feed label with confidence, knowing when you are being buffaloed, and when you are not.

Those of you reading this book, who truly love your horses, will understand immediately what I am talking about. There is a science of reining, and an art of reining. The same is true for racing, jumping, and any of a hundred other disciplines. And so it is with nutrition.

It is the spirit of the horse we love, not the veins and the hormones, and the bones. It is the spirit that draws us to them, again and again, no matter how large, no matter how costly, no matter how dangerous. There is something in the horse, far beyond our meager attempts at analyzing it, that we want for ourselves. And therein lies the core of the art of horsemanship.

By the time you finish reading this book, you will be

able to read any feed label with confidence, knowing when you are being buffaloed, and when you are not. You will be familiar with the major constituents of forages, feeds and supplements, and you will have a good idea how much of each is good for your horse. There will be a lot of science in this book, because science is the language of units and degrees, and any treatise on horse nutrition would be lacking without them. But as you read this book, remember: no one knows your horse as you do, and no one ever will. You may think you bought him for his svelte body and his kind eye, but you really bought him because he was **your** horse; his spirit touched yours. If this book helps you, in some small way, to keep that spirit strong and willing, then it has done its job. And you will have learned quite a bit about the art of horse nutrition.

CHAPTER 2

Feeding as a Function of Design

1888

"The horse was created to live off the grass of the field. This habit necessitated that much ground should be traveled before the appetite of so large a body could be appeased; and the distance was the greater as the animal was sent upon the earth as a nice feeder—biting oft the juicy tops of the herbage, not tearing up roots and all, like the less scrupulous bovine tribe."

DR. EDWARD MAYHEW, *ILLUSTRATED HORSE MANAGEMENT*, 1888

*F*eeding a horse would, intuitively, seem to be a very simple proposition. After all, horses did quite well on their own for several million years before would-be bronze-age horsemen happened upon the historic notion that it might make more sense to feed the horse and let it do the work, than to eat the horse and do the work themselves.

In fact, a maintenance horse kept on good pasture can do quite well with no more additions to the diet than water and salt. But most of us do not have the luxury of good pasture; most horses are kept in stalls with small runs that provide no more in vegetation than the occasional weed to chew on. This means the vast majority of horses are entirely dependent upon humans to provide them with the nutrients they need to grow strong and remain healthy.

By nature, horses are grazers: their natural food of choice is grass. While this fact is evident, it does lead to a couple of conclusions that need to be considered. First, the horse's natural diet has a very high moisture content and, second, it is natural for the horse to eat small amounts of feed on a continual basis. If we contrast these facts with the common feeding practices of today—dry feed given in large amounts one or two times a day—we are left with a glaring disparity between what the horse is built for, and what it is offered. It is no small wonder the leading cause of mortality in horses is colic. The mystery is that most horses do as well as they do.

The horse's stomach is quite small compared to that of its bovine counterpart, the cow. The horse has a single stomach that can hold no more than two to three gallons of liquid, while a cow has a four-part stomach, the first part of which— the rumen—can hold up to 40 gallons. While cows digest most of their feed in the stomach (about 70%), the horse only digests 8% - 9% of its feed there. The bulk of the horse's digestive processes are completed in the small and large intestines. Most of the soluble nutrients are broken down by enzymes and absorbed in the small intestine, while the more insoluble material passes into the large intestine where it is worked on by enzymes produced by colonies of bacteria. This is why horses are referred to as "hindgut fermenters." Problems occur because the large intestine is not of uniform diameter throughout; it contains several bottlenecks and tight, serpentine turns—great places for impaction to occur.

The horse's digestive system is designed to move a continuous stream of moist, fibrous material, and it is very important for us, as their keepers, to approximate those natural conditions as closely as possible. Anyone who has ever spent much time around a large herd of horses knows that they are quite adept at finding ways to block their bowels (sand, rubber fencing, wood chip bedding, etc.) without any help from us.

The basis of any feeding program should be a good quality forage, since horses need to eat 1% to 2% of their body weight (on a dry matter basis) in forage each day.

We lost an excellent race horse to an impaction a few years ago. A postmortem examination revealed a large ball of cords from a rubber fence as the cause of the blockage. The horse was 4-years-old, but he had not been in a pen with that type of fencing since he was a yearling; he had carried that time-bomb with him for three years.

Since most of us cannot pasture our horses year-round, we need to make the best use of what we have. The basis of any feeding program should be a good quality forage, since horses need to eat 1% to 2% of their body weight (on a dry matter basis) in forage each day. For example, an 1100 pound horse needs to eat 11 to 22 pounds of forage daily.

Most hays (alfalfa and grass) contain around 30% fiber on a dry matter basis, much of it insoluble. And even though insoluble fiber provides little in the way of nutrition, it plays an essential role in the dynamics of the digestive system by absorbing water and assisting the flow of material through the gut. In other words, hay re-hydrates in the gut, recreating—as closely as possible—the gastric conditions the horse is anatomically suited to. For older horses, or horses that are hard keepers, beet pulp is an excellent substitute for all or part of a horse's roughage needs. It compares favorably with alfalfa hay in terms of fiber, calcium and digestible energy, though it comes up a bit short on protein (10%) and other nutrients.

Unfortunately, neither beet pulp nor hays are always sufficiently nutrient-laden to supply the horse with everything it needs to be the shiny, healthy animal we so admire.

There is simply not enough energy in most dry forages to meet a horse's enormous nutritional demands. To do that, we need to add concentrated, high-energy feed to the diet; things that are low in fiber. But don't despair; as long as we do this wisely, and bear in mind the horse's digestive limitations, we should be able to minimize any feed-related problems.

> There is simply not enough energy in most hay to meet a horse's enormous nutritional demands. To do that, we need to add concentrated, high-energy feed to the diet; things that are low in fiber.

CHAPTER 3

Energy:
Fuel for the Equine Engine

*E*nergy is required by a horse for every single activity it engages in, from running a race, to digesting its food, to blinking its eyes. When growth or performance falters, many horsemen look for exotic solutions to what might be a very simple problem—namely, the horse's basic energy requirements are not being met. Horses low in energy lose weight and condition, and refuse to work. The growth of young horses is slowed. Mares come into heat later in the season, and can have prolonged gestation periods. And often all that is needed is better quality hay and a little more grain.

All of the energy used by the horse is derived from three classes of nutrients: carbohydrates, fats and proteins. When the chemical bonds that hold these nutrients together are broken, energy is released and work is performed. The energy requirement of horses is

All of the energy used by the horse is derived from three classes of nutrients: carbohydrates, fats and proteins.

expressed as Digestible Energy (DE), which is the energy in its feed minus the energy in its feces. Digestible energy is measured in Mcals (megacalories). *Each Mcal is equal to 1000 calories and, for the sake of simplicity, I have converted Mcals to calories throughout the book.*

Just how much energy does a horse require? An average working horse that eats 19.6 Mcals (19,600 calories) of digestible energy per day consumes enough energy to turn a 55 gallon drum of ice into a boiling cauldron, a fact that really ought to give you a new respect for hay and oats.

How is the food energy from hay and oats turned into energy to warm the body and keep muscles contracting? All living things, from blades of grass to horses, use the same universal compound to provide energy: ATP, or adenosine triphosphate. As the "tri" in triphosphate suggests, the molecule ends with three phosphate groups held tightly together by very high-energy bonds. It is the energy in the final bond that is of particular importance; the energy in that one bond supplies all the energy a horse uses for everything, from chewing its food to running a grueling, head-to-head race.

ATP is continuously broken down and reassembled by two basic modes of respiration to supply the body with needed energy. The quickest of the two, the anaerobic, works without oxygen, while the other, the aerobic, requires oxygen. Without making things too complicated, we'll look at the merits and limitations of each.

Anaerobic Respiration

Anaerobic respiration is performed in twelve steps. Steps one through ten, interestingly, are identical to the fermentation process used in making wine and beer. Sugar, such as glucose in the case of the horse, is broken down into two molecules of lactic acid (or ethanol, in the fermentation of wine and beer). In the process, two molecules of ATP are used to produce four, for a net gain of two molecules of ATP.

Anaerobic respiration is not especially efficient, though it is fast. In an all-out quarter-mile sprint, almost all of the energy supplied to a horse's muscles is by this means. Since the burning of every gram of sugar produces two grams of lactic acid as waste, in a very short time the muscles are overcome with this lactic acid "exhaust," causing them to ache and burn, and become weak.

Aerobic Respiration

Aerobic respiration is far more efficient than anaerobic. One molecule of glucose will produce 36 molecules of ATP, with water and carbon dioxide as the only waste products. In addition to glucose, protein and fat can be used as fuel. The only drawbacks of aerobic respiration are that it is slow and requires oxygen, neither of which is usually a problem for most horses. A fit horse in a race of a mile or more will derive about half of its energy aerobically, an endurance horse on a 50-mile trek even more. And of course, standing in the pasture eating grass is entirely an aerobic activity.

An average working horse that eats 19.6 Mcals (19,600 calories) of digestible energy per day consumes enough energy to turn a 55 gallon drum of ice into a boiling cauldron, a fact that really ought to give you a new respect for hay and oats.

CHAPTER 4

Nutrients
That Supply Energy

1888

"As a matter of economy, nothing should be placed in the manger which is not fit to be appropriated, or is not proper to nourish the strength. Such is the purpose of food: that is not food which does not feed...."

DR. EDWARD MAYHEW, *ILLUSTRATED HORSE MANAGEMENT*, 1888

Carbohydrates

Carbohydrates are the primary source of energy for horses. They are the main constituents of hay and grain, making them the most conspicuous part of a horse's diet. All carbohydrates are composed of three elements: carbon, hydrogen and oxygen. As the word "hydrate" would suggest, the hydrogen and oxygen are in the same 2:1 ratio as water. Plants use sunlight in a photosynthetic process to combine atmospheric carbon dioxide and water into carbohydrates, and return the extra oxygen to the atmosphere, so horses and horsemen can keep on breathing and exhaling carbon dioxide, so plants can go on growing. It's a very nice exchange.

Glucose, or blood sugar, is also the sugar manufactured by plants during photosynthesis. It is a simple sugar with six carbon atoms attached to the equivalent of six molecules of water. When glucose is linked to itself in long chains it forms molecules of glycogen, a polysaccharide, which is to the horse what starch is to the potato: stored food. Glycogen is the primary fuel of the body. It is stored in the muscle cells, the liver, and in fat around the liver, so for most short-term activities there is plenty of fuel around when it is needed.

The fiber that makes up such a large percentage of a horse's diet consists of several types of polysaccharides, all with varying degrees of digestibility. Soluble fiber is easily digested, while insoluble fiber, such as cellulose, is worked on by microflora in the gut, with marginal success.

Fat

Dietary fat consists of a single molecule of glycerol, with three fatty acid molecules attached to it. Once ingested, fat is broken down into its constituent fatty acids, which circulate through the blood and are stored in tissues throughout the body, especially between muscle cells. Like carbohydrates, fats are composed of atoms of carbon, hydrogen and oxygen, but the levels of carbon and hydrogen are much higher. This makes for stronger chemical bonds and more energy released when they are broken, making fat a high-energy nutrient. All fats are soluble in ether, but not water. If you read a feed table looking for "Crude Fat," it may not be there; if not, look for "Ether Extract"—same difference. Ounce for ounce, fat has 2.25 times more energy than carbohydrates or protein.

Although fat is a very small part of most equine diets (both today and in the past when horses roamed the Great Plains), horses do possess a surprising ability to digest it. Many trainers are taking advantage of that fact by adding fat to the diet of their horses in training. Since fat can only be burned aerobically, it is of questionable benefit for horses in an all-out performance, but can help horses during slower, paced activities. Fat is such a concentrated feed that using fat to replace some of the grain in a performance horse's diet can help to achieve a comparable energy balance with less bulk. An ounce of corn oil contains about 255 calories of digestible energy. Corn oil is a very palatable fat for horses, and it can be added to the diet liberally, though there is a point at which a horse will refuse to eat it.

A word of caution, however: if you are feeding a horse several ounces of fat per day, it is important to keep the total

If you read a feed table looking for "Crude Fat," it may not be there; if not, look for "Ether Extract"— same difference. Ounce for ounce, fat has 2.25 times more energy than carbohydrates or protein.

protein in the diet at a high level, since fat does interfere with protein absorption. Try to feed a bare minimum of 12% protein, raising the level in accordance with the horse's work load.

Fatty Acids

There has been a lot of buzz about fatty acids in human nutrition in the past few years, and much of it is beginning to spill over into the realm of horse nutrition. We often hear the terms saturated, unsaturated, and polyunsaturated fat (or fatty acids). Mostly we

There are three fatty acids needed by all animals that no animal can produce on its own...Omega-3, -6, and -9 fatty acids.

are told that saturated fatty acids (those that are primarily derived from animals) are bad for us, and that unsaturated and polyunsaturated fatty acids are better, but not much. Then, just when they've finally got us to the point that the simple act of slathering a slice of bread with butter or margarine causes an anxiety attack, someone comes along and tells us how important it is that we consume adequate amounts of the Omega-3, -6, and -9 fatty acids.

What's going on here? And what's this got to do with what we feed our horses?

It's really quite simple, chemically speaking, so bear with me. Fatty acids are made of chains of carbon and hydrogen. In a saturated fatty acid, each atom of carbon is bonded to two atoms of hydrogen. The resulting molecule is dense, and therefore usually in a solid state at room temperature.

In an unsaturated fatty acid, two side-by-side hydrogen atoms are missing at some point in the chain, causing the two side-by-side carbon atoms to form a double bond between themselves. The molecule is less dense, and is usually a liquid

oil at room temperature. (As you can imagine, a polyunsaturated fatty acid is one where more than one double carbon
bond is present.)

Here's the tricky part: while you may think it wouldn't
matter a whit where in the chain the double carbon bond(s)
exists, in reality it matters a great deal. That's because different fatty acids serve different functions in animal metabolism. Moreover, there are three types of fatty acids needed by
all animals that no animal can produce on its own, namely:
Omega-3, -6, and -9 fatty acids. *The "Omega" refers to the last
carbon on the chain that forms a double bond with its neighbor;
the associated number refers to the position of the first double-
bonded carbon back from the Omega carbon.* Of these, the most
important are linolenic acid and linoleic acid.

Since these three fatty acids are needed by horses—and
people and chickens and fish—you will see a lot of products
that provide them. This is fine, but before you spend a whole
lot of money on specialty products, remember this: that animals can make higher number Omega fatty acids from lower
ones (9 can be made from 6, which in turn can be made from
3), as long as there is enough raw material to work with. So,
if fed enough Omega-3, you shouldn't have to worry about
finding your horse an extra source of Omega-6 and Omega-9.

While the exact requirements for these three essential
fatty acids has not been determined for the horse, most horses on good feed should be getting plenty of each. On the

---

What About Polar Bears?

If polar bears eat only other animals, and those animals don't produce
Omega-3, -6 and -9 fatty acids, where do the big, contrary beasts get
their much needed essential fatty acids? Well, polar bears eat seals,
which eat fish, which eat algae, which are loaded with essential fatty
acids. Thus, the mighty polar bear's Omega fatty acids originate with
lowly single-celled marine plants.

other hand, if your horse has dry skin; weak, brittle hooves; or a lusterless haircoat, you may want to try adding flaxseed meal to the feed. It's extremely rich in Omega-3 and –6 fatty acids. And, unlike other, highly processed oils, the fatty acids in flaxseed haven't been converted to a (decidedly unhealthy) *trans* state, an unnatural molecular arrangement in which pairs of hydrogen atoms have been plucked from both the top and bottom of the chain.

Protein

The body can also burn protein as fuel, after the nitrogen has been removed and the carbon chain has broken down. But like fat, protein can only be burned aerobically, in the presence of oxygen. During a grueling performance,

Protein's main role should not be as a fuel, but as a building material.

when glycogen stores in the muscles are nearly depleted, protein is pulled from nearby muscle cells and burned as fuel if there is no other source of energy available.

As an energy source, protein is not a wise choice. It contains no more energy than carbohydrates, and it is several times more expensive to feed. But there is a lot more to protein than its energy value. Protein's main role should not be as a fuel, but as a building material......

Protein: The Stuff Your Horse Is Made Of

If horses possessed the same abilities as the plants they eat, all we would have to do is feed them a little ammonium nitrate, some simple sugars, and a few trace minerals. With those ingredients they could make all the protein they would ever need, and we could dispense with this section of the book. But evolution is economical; if the plant can do it, the animal eating the plant shouldn't have to. This thrifty arrangement frees up the horse's limited biological resources to be better used in other metabolic processes.

Actually, it is not protein the horse needs, but the amino acids that are the building blocks of protein. Horses make their own protein at the cellular level, if all the right amino acids are available. But while some amino acids are manufactured by bacteria in the hindgut, there are 11 amino acids that either cannot be synthesized, or cannot be synthesized in sufficient quantity, and must be fed to the horse. These are known as essential amino acids. There are about as many amino acids as there are letters in the alphabet (25, or thereabouts) and since proteins are really nothing but long chains of amino acids, there are as many possible proteins as there are combinations of letters. In other words, for all intents and purposes, an endless number.

Proteins are in every cell of the body—they are the very basis of protoplasm. They provide the framework for the structure of the body. Proteins are absolutely necessary for the growth and maintenance of muscle tissue, enzymes, cartilage and connective tissue, blood cells, hooves, hair—you name it: if it's a functional part of the horse, then part of it is protein.

To maintain good health, a horse needs—depending on its stage of life and level of activity—between 8% and 15% protein in the total diet, figured on a dry matter basis. If there is not enough protein in the diet, the horse will develop a dry and lusterless haircoat, a loss of appetite, slow hoof growth and, if the condition goes unchecked, loss of body tissue.

There is a direct correlation between protein and energy: a horse will need between 40 to 50 grams of protein for each

Mcal (1,000 calories) of digestible energy, with the maintenance horse on the low end, and the lactating mare on the high end of the spectrum.

If there is not enough protein in the diet, the horse will develop a dry and lusterless haircoat, a loss of appetite, slow hoof growth and, if the condition goes unchecked, loss of body tissue.

While hay and pasture are the primary sources of protein for the horse, many (if not most) horses will require an additional protein source, depending on the quality of the forage. Good quality alfalfa hay cut in the early stages and put up right, can be as high as 20% protein soon after it is baled, with the protein content slowly dwindling during storage. On the other hand, bromegrass hay can be as little as 5% protein, or as high as 14%, depending on when it is cut, and how it is harvested. Timothy, Bermudagrass and orchardgrass usually contain somewhere between 7% and 13% protein. The earlier hay is cut, and the sooner it is baled, the better.

Cereal grains also contain varying levels of protein. Oats, depending on the grade, are between 9% and 14% protein, barley between 11% and 13%, and corn between 7.5% and 12%. Other sources of protein include soybean meal (45%), cottonseed meal (41%), and linseed meal (35%).

All of these values are for crude protein, not digestible protein. Some proteins are of a higher quality than others. High quality proteins supply more of the amino acids the horse needs, and of **those** proteins, some are more digestible than others. Alfalfa hay that is 18% crude protein, for instance, will be about 13% digestible protein, while a grass hay with 13% crude protein will only be about 7% digestible protein.

Is digestible protein important? Yes, but values for it are difficult to determine. Most feed manuals list protein

If you suspect that none of
these sources is giving your
horse the quality of protein it
needs, supplementation with
lysine can greatly improve
the total protein quality.

concentrations of feed as crude protein. To be on the safe side, you should provide your horse with several protein sources. If you suspect that none of these sources is giving your horse the quality of protein it needs, supplementation with the amino acid, lysine, can greatly improve the total protein quality, as lysine appears to be the most critical of the essential amino acids.

Finally, since so many horsemen are also cattlemen, I should mention non-protein nitrogen sources, such as urea. These compounds are converted into protein, either by the horse itself, or by bacteria in the gut. Although urea has been shown to be of definite benefit to cattle, a horse's digestive machinery is not as adept at making protein as their bovine counterparts. By the same token, a horse's lack of ability to utilize urea gives it a higher tolerance to it, since much of it is excreted before it is converted into toxic levels of ammonia in the hindgut. But is it worth the trouble to feed it? No—the risk of accidental poisoning is too great, and far outweighs any benefit. All this being said, if you still feel the need to tempt fate, there are two things to remember: **urea should not be fed to mature horses at a rate of more than 4% of the total diet, and it should not be fed to young horses, at all**, since they do not possess the same tolerance for it that older horses do.

CHAPTER 5

Putting Things Into Perspective with a Bigger and Better Trojan Horse

---

circa 25 B.C.

"The sides were plank'd with pine; they feign'd it made
For their return, and this the vow they paid.
Thus they pretend, but in the hollow side
Selected numbers of their soldiers hide."

VIRGIL, THE SECOND BOOK OF *THE AENEIS*, CIRCA 25 B.C.

---

*E*veryone has heard of the Trojan War—the 10-year battle between the Greeks of Sparta and the Trojans of Troy (or Ilium). Legend has it that the war began following the abduction of the world's most beautiful woman, and ended after a clever deception, centered around the world's biggest horse. It was a giant steed, fashioned from wood and steel by the battle-weary Greeks, and made hollow to hold the warriors that would sack and burn Troy, once the horse was pulled within the city's walls. Although Virgil, in his epic poem *The Aenid*, never gives the dimensions of the Trojan Horse, it is reputed to have held a thousand warriors. A sizable horse, by any standards. In order to put into perspective the units of measure found on feed labels these days, I am going to propose an even bigger horse—one that is made of flesh and bone (of the imaginary variety). But first we need to become familiar with some common feed industry terminology.

Anyone who has ever taken the time to read the guaranteed analysis on a feed tag, or a bucket of horse supplement, has probably noticed that all of the nutrients are listed in comparative units, such as "mg./lb." or "PPM". Specifically, you will find five such units of measure, if your feed label is printed according to AAFCO (Association of American Feed Control Officers) guidelines and regulations: % (percent), IU/lb., PPM, mg./lb., and mcg./lb. *(The inset on the next page describes these units of measure in detail.)*

If a pound were 1000 miles, a gram would be 2.2 miles; a milligram 11 feet, 8 inches; and a microgram 1/8th of an inch. Interesting, but it's even better in 3-D.

After years of formulating feed supplements and preparing the labels to go with them, it occurred to me that I had no concept of what a part-per-million or a milligram-per-pound was, in everyday, familiar terms. It is easy enough to do the math and learn that one particular unit is such and such a fraction of another, but to really comprehend the meaning of the numbers requires a leap of the imagination.

Since a mastery of these terms is necessary to fully understand the quantities of nutrients going into our horses, I thought it would be helpful to use the Trojan Horse analogy to bring these tiny but essential amounts into the human realm. I will not use percentages, since they speak for themselves, or IU/lb., because the con-

> **Units of Measure on Feed Labels**
>
> **% (percent)**   Used to guarantee protein and amino acids, fat, fiber, and macrominerals, such as calcium, phosphorus, salt, and magnesium.
>
> **IU/lb.**   (International Units per Pound) Used only to guarantee the fat soluble vitamins A, E, and D.
>
> **PPM**   An acronym for "Parts per Million," also equal to milligrams per kilogram. Trace minerals, such as copper, cobalt, zinc, etc. should be guaranteed in PPM.
>
> **mg./lb.**   Milligrams per pound. Used primarily to guarantee the water soluble vitamins, such as thiamin, pyridoxine, niacin, etc. A milligram is 1/453,600th of a pound.
>
> **mcg./lb. (or µg./lb.)**   Micrograms per pound. Sometimes used to express guarantees of minute amounts of certain nutrients such as vitamin B_{12}. A microgram is 1/453,600,000th of a pound.

centration of international units varies from vitamin to vitamin, but PPM, mg./lb., and mcg./lb. are ripe for illumination. Before we go on, it might be helpful to give a one-dimensional analogy: if a pound were 1,000 miles, a gram would be 2.2 miles; a milligram 11 feet, 8 inches; and a microgram 1/8th of an inch. Interesting, but it's even better in 3-D.

To start with, a pound is not the fourth part of a coffee can of grain anymore—it is a room in your house. Let's make this room 12-foot by 12-foot, with an 8-foot ceiling. It may be your bedroom, or perhaps your kitchen (with all of the furniture, cabinets, and appliances removed, please). Now,

what could we put in this big, empty room to represent one PPM?   A cherry tomato is just about
right. Take this conceptual cherry tomato, set it in
the corner, and be happy knowing that you are
only 999,999 cherry tomatoes away from filling your kitchen
with small, red, bullet-proof salad vegetables.

To represent one milligram (a thousandth of a gram) in
our room-sized pound we can go a bit bigger: all the way up
to a large egg. But if we want to demonstrate the size of one
microgram (a millionth of a gram) we have to search around
in the cabinets we just removed to find one, tiny peppercorn.

But remember, our room is just one pound, and a
horse eats several pounds of feed every day. In fact, extend-
ing our analogy, each day our Trojan Horse eats the equivalent of a 2,400 square foot house, full to the rafters with feed.

Just how big is this house-eating horse? From the
ground to the withers, it is 192 feet (or, if you wish, 576
hands). From the tip of its nose to the base of its tail, 328 feet
(or a little longer than a football field). Its legs are over 110
feet long, and 14 feet in diameter at the knees. It could cover
the 1¼ miles of the Kentucky Derby in about five strides.

If we feed this horse 15 milligrams of biotin per day to
maintain its enormous hooves—they span 20 feet—the biotin
would occupy the volume of a mere 15 chicken eggs.

And by the way, if we were to hollow this horse out and
use it as a siege engine, it would hold somewhere in the
neighborhood of 13,200 Greek warriors, or cowboys,
depending on whether we were attacking Troy or Dallas.

Now that we have a clear understanding of the relative
proportions of the units used throughout the book—as well
as on all feed and supplement labels—we can examine the
nutrients that are guaranteed in those units, and how they
apply to different classes of the horse.

CHAPTER 6

The Fundamentals:
Energy & Protein Requirements

1888

"Horses differ quite as much as men do in their appetites. By common practice, one animal receives more than it requires, while another gets less than satisfies its cravings."

DR. EDWARD MAYHEW, *ILLUSTRATED HORSE MANAGEMENT*, 1888

---

*A*nyone who has ever paged through a horse magazine or a mailing from one of the larger catalog houses has no doubt come to the conclusion that it is possible to indulge a horse with an endless variety of feeds and supplements. Every day a new company will pop onto the scene, claiming that they, and they alone, have the solution to all of your horse's problems. It often reminds me of a modern-day version of the traveling medicine show, where tonics were proffered that cured everything from corns to consumption. But the fact is, if you can sort through the fantastic claims being made by a few unscrupulous manufacturers, there really are some very good products on the market that have proven beneficial to thousands of horses. We have learned a lot about nutrition in the past 10 or 20 years, and the result has been a boon to horsemen who have been able to educate themselves enough to sort through the hoopla. Hopefully, after reading this book you will be able to decide what is good for your horse, and what is only good for the manufacturer's bottom line.

For now, though, we will only concern ourselves with the basics; energy and protein, and a few more of the essentials that are critically important to different classes of the horse. As we go through *Part Two: Nutrients That Do Not Supply Energy* (chapters 7 - 9), we will refer back to the horse classes discussed here.

Please note that the requirements listed for the various classes are minimum amounts needed to maintain health.[1] They are not necessarily **optimum** amounts. Certain nutrients, such as calcium and phosphorus should be fed at rates close to the amounts listed, while others, like vitamin A, can

---

1   A mature body weight of 1100 lbs. has been assumed for all horses in the following examples. The nutrient amounts may be adjusted for larger or smaller horses, bearing in mind that—as a general rule—smaller horses require a slightly higher level of nutrients per pound than larger horses.

and probably should be fed at higher levels. If this raises a cloud of confusion, it should dissipate during the discussion of the individual nutrients. The "Guide to Supplemental Feeding" (pages 145 - 147) should further clear the air.

Maintenance Horses

The maintenance horse is an animal who enjoys a blissfully boring life in the pasture, or in a small run behind the house. He spends his days standing in one spot, wondering when dinner will be served, or amuses himself by trying to stretch his neck far enough to reach a few blades of grass on the neighbor's side of the fence. He might be an old gelding that you ride a little on weekends, or a horse injured in competition needing a little rest. An empty mare, or a mare just bred and without foal, fits the maintenance category too. What do these horses need, nutritionally, to keep weight on and their coats shiny, to maintain the gleam in their eyes, and to give you a run for your money when you ride them too close to the fire-breathing Rottweiler your neighbor keeps chained up in his yard? The chart on the right will be a good start.

Although this is only a few of the nutrients known to be necessary to the horse, it covers most of the major ones, and will nicely serve our purpose here. On the next page is a comparison of two types of hay: sun-cured alfalfa in mid-bloom

Daily Needs of 1100 lb. MAINTENANCE HORSE	
Based on Total Dry Feed Intake of 18 lbs. per day	
Digestible Energy	16,400 calories
Crude Protein (8%)	655 g.
Calcium	22 g.
Phosphorus	14 g.
Magnesium	8 g.
Zinc	327 mg.
Copper	82 mg.
Vitamin A	15,000 IU
Vitamin E	409 IU

Comparison of Hay
Based on Total Dry Feed Intake of 18 lbs. per day

	Alfalfa	Bromegrass
Digestible Energy	16,800 calories	14,900 calories
Crude Protein	1526 g.	490 g.
Calcium	111.0 g.	20.7 g.
Phosphorus	19.6 g.	18 g.
Magnesium	28.6 g.	9.8 g.
Zinc	253 mg.	196 mg.
Copper	144 mg.	82 mg.
Vitamin A	376,360 IU	90,000 IU

(this is about as good as hay gets), and sun-cured bromegrass in the late stages of growth, a far more pedestrian type of hay.[2]

And who said that horse nutrition was a difficult subject? Just give that horse a couple of flakes of top-quality alfalfa hay morning and night, plenty of water and salt, and you're home free; nothing could be easier. With the exception of a few milligrams of zinc, the alfalfa hay has everything the horse needs to keep going. The calcium to phosphorus ratio in this hay exceeds 5 to 1, far too high for a growing foal, but marginally acceptable in a mature, maintenance horse. At any rate, the ratio could easily be brought into line by the addition of monosodium phosphate to the salt.

The bromegrass hay, on the other hand, falls a little short of the mark in digestible energy (calories) and far short in protein. To keep that airy little bounce in this horse's step, we need to find a way to get the protein level up and add a few more calories to its diet. Let's add one pound of soybean meal, and three pounds of oats (inset on next page).

---

2 Most of the information in these feed analyses is adapted from the National Research Council's *Nutrient Requirements of Horses,* a must book for any serious student of horse nutrition.

	Bromegrass Hay	Soybean Meal	Oats	Total
Adjusted Ration: Add Soybean Meal & Oats				
To Raise the Protein Level and Number of Calories				
Dry Feed Intake (lbs.)	14	1	3	**18**
Digestible Energy (calories)	10,780	1,600	4,350	**16,730**
Crude Protein (g.)	381	226	181	**788**
Calcium (g.)	16.5	1.8	1.2	**19.5**
Phosphorus (g.)	14	3.2	5.2	**22.4**
Magnesium (g.)	7.6	1.4	2.2	**11.2**
Zinc (mg.)	152	26	53	**231**
Copper (mg.)	66	10	9	**85**
Vitamin A (IU)	74,375	0	60	**74,435**

We are getting a little closer with this ration. Phosphorus is higher than calcium, but should be safe. We have the protein up to over 9%,[3] which is acceptable with a maintenance horse, and enough calories to meet its barest energy demands. Unfortunately, because protein is so expensive, we are now spending nearly as much money on the one

3 See page 152, for the formula to calculate total protein in mixed rations.

pound of soybean meal as we are on the 16 pounds of hay, and they don't give oats away, either. On the other hand, if we add just ½ pound of soybean meal and 5 pounds of oats, fed with 12½ pounds of hay, the protein is still around 9% and we've saved a little money. Of course, we are assuming that the bromegrass hay was put up under the right conditions and stored out of the weather, since rain and sunlight can leach the nutrients out of hay in short order. If this horse was stressed by bad teeth, parasites, poor weather or disease, its nutritional needs would increase sharply. But we have solved a problem arising from poor quality hay, and offered a basic idea of the process of calculating a workable ration. These rations are only two of hundreds of possible rations, any one of which would work equally as well. (Note that zinc is low in every one of these rations and should be supplemented in some form.) Obviously the best solution would be to find better hay, but that is not always possible.

Our maintenance horse would most likely do quite well on one of the bromegrass, oats and soybean meal diets. A lot of horses have prospered on less. Of course, this horse is the easiest of all types of horses to keep; it is finished growing, and doesn't expend much energy to stay alive. As other factors come into play, the art of feeding becomes increasingly more interesting.

Older Horses

While we may not ask more of our older horses than we do of the average maintenance horse, they may ask more from us. If you have a horse that's getting on in years, it's important to make sure it's getting enough nutrition, and of the right sort. Specifically, you should feed this horse only the highest quality hay (palatable, dust-free hay, high in protein), and be certain it's vitamin and mineral requirements are being met. For hard keepers, or horses that tend to colic, beet pulp is a nice addition to, or replacement for, hay. It's high in good quality fiber and easy to chew—though, at 10%, it's a little lower in protein than good-quality hay.

If possible, smaller amounts of feed, given more frequently, are less stressful than one or two big feedings per day. There are several feeds on the market specifically for older ("senior," I believe, is the word) horses, that are palatable and high in the nutrients most needed by our aging companions.

Performance Horses

Performance horses are the hearty steeds that capture the imaginations of everyone—horsemen and non-horsemen alike. They are the sleek competitors in the Triple Crown races, the muscular acrobats in Britain's Grand National, and the stocky speedsters in the All American Futurity. But they also include the marathon

Daily Needs of 1100 lb. PERFORMANCE HORSE	
Based on Total Dry Feed Intake of 25.3 lbs. per day	
Digestible Energy	32,700 calories
Crude Protein (11.4%)	1309 g.
Calcium	40 g.
Phosphorus	29 g.
Magnesium	15.1 g.
Zinc	459 mg.
Copper	115 mg.
Vitamin A	22,453 IU
Vitamin E	919 IU

runners of endurance races so popular in the American West, and the hard-working roping and barrel horses in American rodeos; they are the trotters and the walkers and the chariot racers. Everyday these horses try to win against the best of the best, and the nutrition they are provided is one-third of the winning equation, equal in importance to training and genetics.

Entire books have been written on the subject of feeding the performance horse, and it would be folly for me to try
to condense even a fraction of that knowledge into a few
short pages. There are as many nutritional formulas for winning competitions as there are nutritionists. But any feeding
program that is worth its salt begins with energy. If the performance horse lacks energy, everything else is academic.

The energy requirements of a horse in heavy training
are easily double those of a maintenance horse. While the
dietary energy needed by a maintenance horse is around
16,400 calories per day, a horse at the track on a demanding
racing schedule can easily burn up 32,000 calories daily or
more. It would take over 45 pounds of the late-stage
bromegrass hay we analyzed earlier to supply that much energy, or 36 pounds of high-grade alfalfa hay. Obviously, this is
not acceptable, even if a horse could eat that much hay (and
I'm sure we've all seen a few that could). A more concentrated source of energy is required, such as a mixture of corn
and oats. While corn is a very high-energy feed, it is extremely low in fiber which, you will remember, is a critical part of
a horse's diet. To ensure, therefore, that fiber is not lacking,
it's a good policy to combine oats and corn in a 1:1 ratio. The
following diet should safely supply the energy needs of an
1100 lb. race horse:

High Quality Alfalfa Hay (14 lbs., dry)	14,500 calories
Corn (7 lbs., dry)	12,200 calories
Oats (7 lbs., dry)	10,150 calories
Total	**36,850 calories**

But what about protein? If high-quality hay is fed (and
by that I mean hay that is in the 18% – 19% range), the total
ration will be around 14% – 15% protein, which will be plenty. Unfortunately, this type of hay is not easy to find. Hay in

the 10% – 13% range is more the norm, which means an additional protein source may be required, such as soybean meal or cottonseed meal. Many feed mills carry fortified sweet feeds in the 12% – 16% range. The better feeds contain a liberal sprinkling of essential vitamins and minerals.

While it is a good practice to put as much hay in the diet as possible, many owners and trainers feed only 20% of the ration as hay, making up the difference with oats, corn, barley, molasses, fat, soybean meal, and various mixtures of vitamins and minerals. Such a small amount of hay can be dangerous, and is not recommended.

Just as the energy needs of a performance horse can be double those of a maintenance horse, the need for other nutrients increases too, but not necessarily on a one-to-one basis. The requirement for some nutrients, such as vitamin E, more than doubles, while others, like copper, increase by less than half. And even if the nutritional needs were simply an arithmetic progression, we cannot practically feed a performance horse twice the amount we feed a maintenance horse. A high-quality ration, sensibly fortified with vitamins and minerals is a must. Differences between individual horses that may appear slight under normal conditions, are often magnified when horses are stressed by heavy training schedules. Some horses lose weight, no matter what they are fed, others refuse to eat. Many of these problems are nutritionally related conditions, peculiar to each individual horse, and most can be solved by the right feeding regimen.

A horse just coming out of competition and reduced to maintenance horse status should be let down slowly. This horse is sleek and muscular, and constantly on the move. It's as high as a kite. It likes being fast and powerful, and likes its feed. It would be a mistake to make immediate and drastic changes in this horse's diet. The feed should be taken away slowly, over a period of weeks. Once the horse has calmed down and adjusted to its new life, it will need only maintenance levels of nutrition until the next training season.

There are several nutrients beyond those ordinarily found in hay and sweet feed that can be beneficial to performance horses. Each of these nutrients will be discussed in *Part Two: Nutrients That Don't Supply Energy.* You may also refer to the supplementation tables on pages 146 and 147.

Stallions

I have always found stallions to be the most fascinating of horses. In stallions, the human emotions of jealousy and possessiveness are laid bare, free of posturing and pretense. Stallions make it quite clear what they want, and what they are willing to do to get it. They are hell on fences and—should one happen to get loose—other horses. Anyone who has ever seen two antagonistic stallions accidentally end up in the same pen will agree: a stallion fight is a singular event of enormous power and fearsome savagery, in which the two combatants will fight until one or both lie prostrate on the ground, having not even the energy left to stand.

All of this hormone-driven passion carries a price tag. My Thoroughbred stallion needs twice the sweet feed my old gelding needs to maintain his weight, even in the fall, long after the end of breeding season. The stallion devours minerals that the gelding turns his nose up at. Statistically, the stallion should not need all that extra feed. In fact, a stallion's estimated nutritional requirements are all only about 12% – 15% above a maintenance horse of the same weight.

The wild card with stallions is energy. The NRC estimates that an 1100 pound breeding stallion should have a minimum of 20,500 calories in the diet. Some high-strung stallions will wither away with that little energy, others will do quite well. It is important to keep a stallion in good condition, neither too fat nor too thin. Routine exercise can help keep the stallion in condition, and take his mind off the duties he so amorously pursues—for a time, anyway. Occasionally a stallion will develop the same problems some track horses do: excessive nervousness and loss of appetite. The addition of thiamin (vitamin B_1) to the feed can usually help such horses.

Keep a watchful eye on your stallion. Watch his feed, his performance, and his condition. He depends on you for his health and his livelihood, just as you depend on him for the results of his charged libido.

Daily Needs of 1100 lb.
BREEDING STALLION
Based on Total Dry Feed Intake
of 18.8 lbs. per day

Digestible Energy	20,500 calories
Crude Protein (9.6%)	818 g.
Calcium	25 g.
Phosphorus	18 g.
Magnesium	9.4 g.
Zinc	341 mg.
Copper	86 mg.
Vitamin A	22,453 IU
Vitamin E	682 IU

Broodmares

Just like expectant human mothers, the nutritional needs of broodmares change over time. The difference is that they cannot run to the local convenience store at midnight to procure the nutrients they need in a bizarre collage of junk foods—they have to rely on you to feed them everything they need for their foals to be born healthy, and to stay that way. It is your responsibility to keep a watchful eye on your mare to be certain that she stays in condition—neither too fat nor too thin, with a healthy haircoat and plenty of energy.

The nutritional needs of a pregnant mare without a nursing foal at side are the same as for a maintenance horse for the first few months. But by the eighth or ninth month, her nutritional needs will rise sharply. The foal inside her is growing at a geometric rate, and if she is not given enough of what she requires to sustain that growth, she will pull nutrients out of her own tissues to ensure growth continues. At this point, minerals are of paramount importance. While her energy needs will increase by only 15% – 20%, her needs for calcium and phosphorus will nearly double. To the left are some of the daily nutritional requirements for an 1100 pound mare in the third trimester of pregnancy.

Once the mare foals and begins producing 20 to 30 pounds of milk per day, she will need 40% – 50% more digestible energy, and

Daily Needs of 1100 lb. PREGNANT MARE (3rd Trimester) Based on Total Dry Feed Intake of 18 lbs. per day	
Digestible Energy	19,600 calories
Crude Protein (10.6%)	865 g.
Calcium	38 g.
Phosphorus	28 g.
Magnesium	9.4 g.
Zinc	327 mg.
Copper	82 mg.
Vitamin A	29,940 IU
Vitamin E	655 IU

70% – 80% more calcium and phosphorus than she did before parturition. Although she will need more energy at this time, care should be taken during the first week to ten days after foaling not to give the mare so much grain that the foal develops milk scours.

Next are a mare's daily requirements for these same nutrients, after the foal is born.

By the time the foal is ready to be weaned, the mare will probably be wondering how she ever let herself get into this predicament in the first place; she'll be tired and worn, and might even be showing a few ribs. Just the same, you should cut back on the grain a week before and a week after weaning. This will help the foal adjust to being weaned, and will ensure that the mare is not turned out with a painfully full udder.

Daily Needs of 1100 lb. LACTATING MARE	
Based on Total Dry Feed Intake of 23.9 lbs. per day	
Digestible Energy	28,200 calories
Crude Protein (13.11%)	1425 g.
Calcium	56 g.
Phosphorus	36 g.
Magnesium	10.9 g.
Zinc	434 mg.
Copper	108 mg.
Vitamin A	29,940 IU
Vitamin E	870 IU

Nursing Foals

For a new foal, the act of being born is like awakening from a deep sleep inside a life-support incubator on a warm and cozy spaceship, and being cast naked onto a cold and hostile planet. Its supply of perfectly nourishing food has been severed and it must very quickly learn to feed itself, or perish. For the first few days, it is content to drink Mother's milk, but after a week or so curiosity leads it to sample the interesting selection of feeds its mother eats with such prejudicial

Daily Needs of 340 lb. 3-MONTH-OLD FOAL

Based on Total Dry Feed Intake of 9.6 lbs. per day

Digestible Energy	12,700 calories
Crude Protein	633 g.
Calcium	33 g.
Phosphorus	18 g.
Magnesium	3.5 g.
Zinc	174 mg.
Copper	44 mg.
Vitamin A	7,000 IU
Vitamin E	350 IU
Ave. gain per day	*1.80 lb.*

single-mindedness.

Soon inquisitiveness about Mother's food turns to desire, then to need. By three weeks of age the foal is growing so rapidly that its mother cannot possibly supply it with the nutrients needed to continue this explosive stage of growth. If the mare is on pasture, the foal can graze at will, and steal a little of whatever other feed the mare is getting. If the mare is penned up, the foal can eat as much hay as the mare will let it have. Either way, you now have to ask yourself if the foal is getting everything it needs to sustain growth, or if extra feed—creep feed—sequestered away from the mare and available only to the foal, is necessary.

I know that many horsemen are opposed to creep feeding, and I can only suppose that they have had bad experiences of one kind or another, or simply have heard of someone who did. But I have creep fed hundreds of foals over the last 25 years, and have never seen one that was harmed in any way

because of it. A foal that is given creep feed will grow 20% – 25% faster than one left to fend for itself, and if the ration is balanced, it will suffer no ill-effects from this accelerated growth.

The goal of creep feeding is to give the foal the nutrients needed to grow strong and remain healthy, not just to give it more food. To simply feed the foal more energy (as carbohydrates or fat) without meeting its protein or mineral requirements can, indeed, have unpleasant consequences. You could end up with a chubby foal on weak legs, with swollen joints, or worse. But with the right creep feed, you should see your investment paid back with interest. The question is: what does the foal need?

The foal may be less than one-third the size of the maintenance horse, but it needs 78% as much energy, as much protein, 50% **more** calcium, and 25% **more** phosphorus. How much of this is supplied by its mother's milk?

What Does A Foal Need In Addition To Milk?			
	Needed by Foal	Supplied in Milk*	Deficit
Digestible Energy	12,700 cal.	7,000 cal.	**5,700 cal.**
Crude Protein	633 g.	286 g.	**347 g.**
Calcium	33 g.	14 g.	**19 g.**
Phosphorus	18 g.	7 g.	**11 g.**
* Average supplied in 30 pounds of Mother's milk			

Even after drinking 30 pounds of its mother's milk, the foal still needs more calories and calcium, plus over half the protein and nearly as much phosphorus as an 1100 pound maintenance horse needs. It would take a very accomplished sneak-thief to steal that much nutrition away from a ravenous mother trying desperately to consume enough feed to keep up her end of the foal feeding program.

Supplying the foal with its source of feed is a simple enough thing to do. All it takes is a pen (creep feeder) that is accessible to the foal, but not the mare. The one I use is made from four panels constructed from 1½ inch pipe, 55 inches high. Three of the panels are 16 feet, the fourth is only 14 feet, the gap to the other panel being spanned with a single pipe on the top and bottom. This leaves a 2-foot opening the foal can easily walk through, but one that is too small for the mare. A round feeder placed in the middle of this enclosure contains the creep feed. A creep feeding pen of this size can easily accommodate six foals at a time.

Now all that remains is to determine what should go in the feeder. To do that, you should have a fair idea of the quality of forage the foal is getting, which may mean testing your hay or pasture for digestible energy, protein, calcium, and phosphorus, since these are the most critical nutrients at this stage of the foal's life.

If you have good forage with plenty of energy and protein, there is no point in feeding a lot of extra energy the foal doesn't need. Check with your local feedmills to see what they have available. A partial guaranteed analysis of a 16% protein feed is included in the next section on weanlings and yearlings. Most feedmills carry comparable concentrates. Some feedmills carry 30% – 33% protein supplements that have less energy per pound and is fed at a much lower rate than the 16% feed. You may want to look at this type of supplement if you have good quality forage.

If the hay or pasture is more on the average side, you should offer the foal a less concentrated feed with a higher ratio of energy to protein, and feed more of it. A 14% or 16% protein feed, with 1,400 to 1,500 calories of digestible energy, is often fed at the rate of one pound per day, per month of age. This amount can be adjusted up or down, depending on the quality of forage. Many breeders offer creep feed free-choice, but most of the time the foal will only eat the recommended amount, anyway.

Feeds vary from area to area. The two important things to know are what your foal needs, and what it is getting from the forage and its mother's milk. Look in the next section on weanlings and yearlings for a general analysis of several types of forage. Once you subtract what it is getting from what it needs, just add to the creep feeder what remains. If you have several foals, it should be no problem to get a feedmill to make a custom mix for you, if you provide them with an analysis of what you need.

Weanlings, Yearlings & Beyond

Next to the act of being born, weaning is the most stressful event in a young horse's life. It is also a stressful—and sleepless—time for the horseman who is not able to pen up the mares and foals beyond earshot of the bedroom window.

Even though the nutrient value of its mother's milk has been slowly declining, and the foal has been relying more and more on forages and concentrates for its nutritional needs, at weaning time a very large fraction is removed from the nutritional equation, and the foal will undoubtedly

Daily Needs of 475 lb.
6-MONTH-OLD WEANLING
(Adult Weight 1100 lbs.)
Based on Total Dry Feed Intake
of 11.7 lbs. per day

Digestible Energy	15,300 calories
Crude Protein (14.5%)	767 g.
Calcium	31 g.
Phosphorus	16 g.
Magnesium	4.1 g.
Zinc	212 mg.
Copper	53 mg.
Vitamin A	9,700 IU
Vitamin E	425 IU
Ave. gain per day	*1.50 lb.*

suffer some setback.

If the foal has been creep fed with a good quality concentrate, the drop in the foal's performance will be minimal, because the nutrition supplied from the mare's milk will not have been as nutritionally significant as with the non-creep-fed foal. Nonetheless, after weaning, foals should be watched carefully for abnormalities of growth, gait, and general appearance, because this is the most probable time for nutritionally related problems to occur. The foal is, and has been, growing very quickly—by the time a foal is 6-months-old, it should have reached 45% of its adult weight, and 83% of its adult height. If the foal's body needs something that is in short supply, it will not stop growing. Rather, it will simply use more of what is at hand. It is kind of like framing a wall with 1x8's when the plans call for 2x4's; you may get the wall built, but it is doubtful you will be happy with the results.

The nutritional requirements of the foal do not change on the day of weaning, but the ration should change since the mare's milk has been removed from it. Let's look at the daily needs of a rapidly growing, 6-month-old weanling (inset above), and then decide how to meet those needs. *As always, these values are estimates, calculated for a weanling with a probable mature weight of 1100 pounds, and not unduly stressed by temperature extremes, disease, injury or parasites.*

TABLE A: Typical Nutrient Values of Bluegrass Pasture and Hay					
	Pasture	Alfalfa	Brome	Timothy	Orchard
DE (cals/lb.)	950	940	850	800	880
Protein (g/lb.)	79	77	58	39	52
Calcium (g/lb.)	2.25	5.6	1.13	1.9	1.08
Phosphorus (g/lb.)	2.0	1.0	1.13	0.9	1.36
Zinc (mg/lb.)	13	12.7	11.8	17.3	16.3
Copper (mg/lb.)	7.1	7.3	10.0	6.4	7.6

Table A lists the nutrient values for bluegrass pasture, and four different types of hay, on a dry matter basis. These values can vary substantially from region to region. If there are any peculiar soil conditions in your area that would affect the nutrient content of pasture or hay, your county extension agent would be able to tell you.

Now let's see where we are when we add concentrated feed (Table B) to the ration of 8 pounds of alfalfa/bromegrass hay (Table C on the next page).

TABLE B: Partial Analysis of Concentrated (16% Protein) Feed		
		On Feed Label
Digestible Energy	1440 cal/lb.	1.44 Mcals/lb.
Protein (16%)	72.64 g/lb.	16%
Calcium	4.7 g/lb.	1.03%
Phosphorus	3.6 g/lb.	0.79%
Zinc	54.5 mg/lb.	120 PPM
Copper	18.2 mg/lb.	40 PPM

This is not in the least unwieldy. We have enough energy, and the levels of zinc and copper are well within accepted limits. There should also be enough phosphorus to balance the calcium. Of course, this is just a partial list of the nutrients needed by the weanling. The requirements for the other nutrients will be discussed in the chapters on vitamins and minerals.

As the weanling grows into a yearling and then into a

TABLE C: Adjusted Ration of Hay and Concentrated Feed
To Raise the Number of Calories and Nutrient Values

	4 lb. Alfalfa	4 lb. Brome	6.5 lb. Concentrate	18.5 lb. Total
Dig. Energy (calories)	3,760	3,400	9,360	**16,520**
Crude Protein (g.)	308.0	238.0	472.2	**1018.2**
Calcium (g.)	22.4	4.5	30.6	**57.5**
Phosphorus (g.)	4.0	4.5	23.4	**31.9**
Zinc (mg.)	50.8	47.2	354.1	**452.1**
Copper (mg.)	29.2	40.0	118.0	**187.2**

2-year-old, it will need more and more nutrients, but—since the volume of feed is now greater—the concentration of those nutrients is reduced (see tables on next page). At 12 months the horse is eating half-again as much feed as the weanling, but only needs about a quarter more energy and protein, and just a little more calcium, phosphorus, zinc and copper. You might want to consider, at this point, feeding a less concentrated feed, such as a 14% mix, or even a 12% feed, if your hay is of good enough quality.

The goal should be to sustain steady growth. By age two, the rate of growth has slowed to one third of that for the yearling, and the requirements for calcium, phosphorus, protein and digestible energy have also decreased, at least for horses not in training (see table for comparison).

From age two on, then, the horse's nutrient requirements will be dictated more by its training regimen, than its age or (greatly diminished) rate of growth, and feeding programs should be designed accordingly.

Daily Needs of Growing Horses
(Adult Weight 1100 lbs.)

Age	12-months	18-months	18-months in training
Body Weight	715 lb.	880 lb.	880 lb.
Daily Gain	1.25 lb.	.77 lb.	.77 lb.
Dry Feed Intake	15.7 lb.	17.5 lb.	22 lb.
Digestible Energy	19,900 cal.	19,800 cal.	26,500 cal.
Crude Protein	900 g.	890 g.	1192 g.
Calcium	32 g.	27 g.	36 g.
Phosphorus	17 g.	15 g.	20 g.
Magnesium	6 g.	6.5 g.	8.6 g.
Zinc	285 mg.	317 mg.	400 mg.
Copper	71 mg.	80 mg.	100 mg.
Vitamin A	14,600 IU	18,000 IU	17,962 IU
Vitamin E	600 IU	650 IU	800 IU

Daily Needs of Growing Horses
(Adult Weight 1100 lbs.)

Age	24-months	24-months in training	30-months	30-months in training
Body Weight	990 lb.	990 lb.	1010 lb.	1010 lb.
Daily Gain	.44 lb.	.44 lb.	.25 lb.	.25 lb.
Dry Feed Intake	16.9 lb.	21.8 lb.	15.6 lb.	20.7 lb.
Digestible Energy	18,800 cal.	26,200 cal.	17,300 cal.	24,900 cal.
Crude Protein	800 g.	1115 g.	735 g.	1060 g.
Calcium	24 g.	34 g.	22 g.	32 g.
Phosphorus	13 g.	19 g.	12 g.	18 g.
Magnesium	7 g.	10 g.	7 g.	10 g.
Zinc	307 mg.	396 mg.	283 mg.	380 mg.
Copper	77 mg.	99 mg.	70 mg.	94 mg.
Vitamin A	20,200 IU	20,200 IU	20,600 IU	20,600 IU
Vitamin E	615 IU	800 IU	570 IU	750 IU

CHAPTER 7

Enzymes: Catalysts of Life

*T*hough it is not my intention to give a short course on biological science, I will mention enzymes so often in the following pages that I thought it a subject worthy of expansion. It is included here because many enzymes require minerals and vitamins for activation, and a brief discussion of the importance of enzymes might further our appreciation of the vital roles of these elusive nutrients.

While temperature extremes on the earth's surface range between -128°F to 136°F, our bodies, and those of our horses, must be maintained within a much smaller range. Yet many of the chemical reactions that take place within the body are very high-energy reactions that—when performed in the laboratory—require temperatures and pressures that would kill any horse (or rider) in a heartbeat. Simply put, you cannot stir up starch and water in a test tube at 100 degrees Fahrenheit and expect to get sugar. So how do we do it?

The answer is enzymes. Enzymes are catalysts of life, and they are very specific for the reactions they facilitate. Thousands of different enzymes exist in the body, each assigned to its own special task. They are proteins that rely on a very specific shape and configuration of atoms to work. But how do they work? The key is their shape, which is to say that their shapes are the keys. Whenever an enzyme binds two molecules together, or breaks the bond between them, it fits them together in a chemical

Without enzymes there would be neither digestion of food nor absorption of nutrients. Energy metabolism would grind to a halt. Growth and body maintenance would be impossible. And without minerals and vitamins, all of these enzymes would be immobilized.

embrace like a multi-dimensional key in an impossibly complex lock. Nearly every time a chemical bond is formed or broken—millions of times per second in a horse—it is made possible by the presence of an enzyme. Without enzymes there would be neither digestion of food nor absorption of nutrients. Energy metabolism would grind to a halt. Growth and body maintenance would be impossible. And without minerals and vitamins, all of these enzymes would be immobilized.

Some of the Nutrients Involved In Enzyme Activity

Minerals	Vitamins
Calcium (Ca)	Riboflavin
Magnesium (Mg)	Niacin
Copper (Cu)	Pantothenic Acid
Manganese (Mn)	Pyridoxine
Zinc (Zn)	Biotin
Selenium (Se)	Thiamin

CHAPTER 8

Minerals: Elemental Necessities

> ## 1948
>
> "For the various life processes, not only must there be sufficient supplies of the various essential minerals, but also there must not be a large excess of any of them."
>
> FRANK B. MORRISON, *FEEDS AND FEEDING: 21ST EDITION, 1948*

All of the nutrients we have discussed to this point consist almost exclusively of carbon, hydrogen, oxygen and nitrogen which, interestingly, are all components of common atmospheric gases: carbon dioxide (CO_2), water vapor (H_2O) and nitrogen gas (N_2). Does this mean a horse derives its energy out of thin air? Well not directly, but it is interesting to note that about 93% of the dry mass of green plants is derived not from the soil, but from the atmosphere. Plants—with the help of sunlight and water—**do** turn air into food, and in that sense we could say that what is energy for the horse today was thin air yesterday.

Now we dip further into the periodic table to the more earthy elements known as minerals. There is not much that goes on in a horse's body without the assistance of minerals. Without minerals, the carbohydrates, fats and proteins in the feed could not be converted into muscle, blood, bone or ligaments. Most vitamins, which act as catalysts in the body, require minerals to work.

A horse receiving an ample supply of minerals will require less feed and perform at a higher level than a horse that is not. With minerals, a horse will have a greater resistance to disease. Energy levels and reproductive efficiency will be increased. Mares will cycle earlier in the year, conceive more quickly, and be more apt to carry their foals to term. They will produce more milk, and their foals will grow larger faster and exhibit stronger, denser bone.

Plants do not absorb minerals from the atmosphere, although some minerals, such as sulfur and phosphorus, are found in certain gases in the air. Minerals are unique among the nutrients. Since they are elements, they are indestructible (except at nuclear energies far beyond the range of horse and horseman). Yet even though they cannot be destroyed in the way that carbohydrates, fats, and proteins can, minerals can be moved from place to place, like from the hayfield to the muck bucket, and often they do not find their way back (more on this later). Many minerals act exactly like vitamins, since they are part of enzymes or coenzymes, but minerals are elemental and inorganic, while vitamins are organic compounds made up primarily from the atmospheric gases we mentioned earlier. Vitamins can be manufactured, minerals cannot—they can only be found, or lost.

In the following pages you will see, again and again, that too much of one mineral will interfere with the absorption of another. Minerals must be balanced in the ration. If they are not, a cascading effect of imbalances may occur and virtually every system in the body will be affected. The horse has relatively high tolerance ranges for some minerals, such as copper and zinc. Other minerals, like iron and selenium,

A horse receiving an ample supply of minerals will require less feed and perform at a higher level than a horse that is not. With minerals, a horse will have a greater resistance to disease. Energy levels and reproductive efficiency will be increased.

are not so forgiving. The prudent horseman will always consider individual minerals in context to every other mineral in the ration. It may not be easy, but the results will be well-worth the trouble.

The reference chart on page 99 give the daily mineral requirements for several classes of the horse, and should be a useful guide for those who are considering supplemental minerals.

THE MACROMINERALS

> ### 1948
>
> *"It has been found in recent years that there are large areas of this and other countries where stock suffer seriously from a deficiency of phosphorus in pasturage, hay, and other feeds."*
>
> FRANK B. MORRISON, *FEEDS AND FEEDING: 21ST EDITION*, 1948

Of the over twenty minerals known to be needed by the horse, seven are termed macrominerals, because they are needed in relatively large quantities. The remaining are termed microminerals, or simply trace minerals (or trace elements), since they are needed in only trace amounts. The seven macrominerals are: calcium, phosphorus, magnesium, sodium and chloride (salt), potassium, and sulfur.

Calcium (Ca) and Phosphorus (P)
Searching for the Illusive Balance.

Short of beating your horse's legs with a shovel, there is really no better way to ruin a good, young horse than to feed it a diet with a skewed calcium to phosphorus ratio. I have talked to, and corresponded with, hundreds of horse owners over the years who had problems caused by an imbalance of calcium and phosphorus; and almost invariably their problem was the result of too much calcium in relation to the phosphorus. The most common symptom is swollen knees and fetlock joints in young horses, a condition usually referred to as epiphysitis, or simply physitis. It's a result of a pathological transformation of cartilage into bone. Epiphysitis can be caused by either too much phosphorus or calcium, though calcium is the usual culprit. If the problem is not too far advanced, balancing the calcium and phosphorus in the diet will reverse the symptoms in a few weeks. Occasionally, a mare will produce so much milk that the high calcium content will induce a case of epiphysitis. If this occurs, the mare's energy ration should be cut back to slow milk production and/or the foal should be supplemented with phosphorus. If possible, it might be advisable to wean the foal early.

Feeding too little calcium can be every bit as dangerous, causing conditions known as rickets, where the skeleton becomes weak and deformed, or Miller's Disease (Big Head Disease) where bones of the face, particularly along the jaws and nasal passages, become enlarged. The point is, horses need lots of both calcium and phosphorus, and in a ratio that does not supply too much of one over the other.

What is the magic ratio, and why is it so hard to reach it? Well, conventional wisdom holds that a 2:1 ratio of calcium to phosphorus in the feed is a safe number, and if we need a number to hang our hats on, that is as good as any. According to the NRC (National Research Council), adult horses can tolerate a ratio as high as 5:1, while growing horses are not harmed by a 3:1 ratio. These ratios are workable, providing that there is sufficient phosphorus in the diet. On the other hand, I know of no horse that ever suffered any harm from calcium or phosphorus when given adequate

amounts within the 1:1 to 2:1 range, and the NRC suggests
that this is the optimum range.

Why is it so hard to reach a ratio of such broad tolerance? A look at what many horsemen feed their horses should
shed some light on the problem. Hay is the major part of the
diet, and a large percentage of horsemen feed alfalfa hay, or
an alfalfa/grass mix. Alfalfa hay is a major source of calcium;
some is as much as eight times richer in calcium than phosphorus, and a 6:1 ratio is not at all uncommon. Cereal grains,
such as oats, corn and barley, on the other hand, usually favor
phosphorus by 2:1. The problem is, most horses are fed a lot
more hay than grain, and grain contains so little of each that it
can do little to reestablish the proper balance.

Short of beating your horse's legs with a shovel, there is really no better way to ruin a good, young horse, than to feed it a diet with a skewed calcium to phosphorus ratio.

Supplement manufactur-
ers do little to help the situation. They are well aware of the
coveted 2:1 ratio, and most
supplements are formulated
accordingly, rather than taking
into account the excess calcium
coming from most hays. Unfortunately, horses (and dogs
and cats) are forced to ride the tides of human nutritional
fads and, for reasons I can only imagine, calcium has become
the darling of food manufacturers, while phosphorus is
thought to be something wooden matches are made from. It
is no exaggeration to say that every time someone on Wall
Street touts the value of some human food or supplement
fortified with calcium, a young horse suffers.

The Functions of Calcium

A horse's body is about 2% calcium, while the skeleton is almost 35% calcium. Calcium is absorbed more efficiently than most other minerals, including phosphorus. Absorption rates vary between 50% – 70%, with the ability to absorb calcium declining with age. Calcium from inorganic sources, such as dicalcium phosphate or limestone[1] (calcium carbonate) are better absorbed than from the organic sources found in forages and grains. Calcium absorption can be negatively affected by excess phosphorus, and oxalate, a compound found in most plants in small quantities. Russian Thistle, which grows well in hay fields and often ends up in hay, can contain toxic amounts of oxalate. Phytate, a substance found in many plants, can also reduce calcium absorption. This is especially important for those who like to give their horses bran mashes, since bran is high in phytate.

Besides its major role in bone formation, calcium is also required for:
- Muscular contraction
- Blood clotting
- Normal release of hormones
- Activation of enzymes
- Normal heart rhythm

On the next page are some common grains and forages and the amount of each that should contain around 22 grams of calcium, the amount needed by an average maintenance horse.

---

1 Limestone is, technically speaking, an organic compound, since it contains the element carbon. However, since the calcium is not bound to an organic substrate, such as an amino acid, protein, or polysaccharide, it is considered inorganic within the feed industry.

To get 22 grams of Calcium (Ca), you would need to feed <u>one</u> of the following each day:	
3.9 lbs.	Alfalfa hay (1.24% calcium)
11.3 lbs.	Timothy hay (0.43% calcium)
19.4 lbs.	Bromegrass hay (0.25% calcium)
60.6 lbs.	Oats (0.08% calcium)
97.0 lbs.	Corn (0.05% calcium)
97.0 lbs.	Barley (0.05% calcium)

As I said earlier, cereal grains do not have an abundance of calcium! Conversely, alfalfa hay is loaded with it, so if you are feeding alfalfa hay, and a lot of it, it would be wise to either feed some grass hay along with it, or to supplement with a good source of inorganic phosphorus (preferably monosodium phosphate, which is 26% phosphorus, and supplies 7.37 grams of phosphorus per ounce). On the other hand, if you are feeding grass hay with plenty of grain, you may have to supplement calcium with an inorganic source, such as limestone or dicalcium phosphate.

The Functions of Phosphorus

While most of the phosphorus absorbed by a horse goes into the skeleton (which is 14% – 17% phosphorus), phosphorus is needed for many other functions in the body, including:
- Fat and carbohydrate metabolism
- Repair and growth of cells
- Production of energy (ATP)
- Calcium and sugar metabolism
- Utilization of vitamins
- Kidney function
- Muscle activity

Phosphorus is not as easily absorbed as calcium. A good estimate for the absorption rate of phosphorus is in the range of 30% – 55%. Like calcium, phosphorus is absorbed better by younger horses than mature horses, and is more likely to be absorbed if it is derived from an inorganic source, such as monosodium phosphate. Most phosphorus absorption takes place in the hindgut, with the assistance of bacteria. Therefore, the absorption of phosphorus can be assisted by supplementing feed with certain bacteria enhancing agents, such as yeast culture, or by feeding the bacteria culture itself (e.g., lactobacillus acidophilus). It may not be advisable to feed the bacteria culture for extended periods of time, but rather only to debilitated horses, or horses under severe stress. There is no point in doing for the horse what the horse can normally do for itself.

Below is how much it would take of each of these grains and forages to supply 14 grams of phosphorus, an ample daily ration for a maintenance horse. The far right column shows what percentage of the maintenance level requirement of calcium (22 grams) is supplied by each of these feeds.

**To get 14 grams of Phosphorus (P),
you would need to feed one of the following each day:**

		also provides:
14 lbs.	Alfalfa hay (.22% phosphorus)	*359% Calcium**
15 lbs.	Timothy hay (.20% phosphorus)	*132% Calcium**
12 lbs.	Bromegrass hay (.25% phosphorus)	*62% Calcium**
9 lbs.	Oats (.34% phosphorus)	*15% Calcium**
11 lbs.	Corn (.27% phosphorus)	*12% Calcium**
9 lbs.	Barley (.34% phosphorus)	*10% Calcium**

Percent of Calcium Requirement, based on 22 grams/day.

Obviously, it takes a very large amount of grain to supply enough phosphorus to balance out the calcium in alfalfa hay; probably more than most horsemen need to feed. A sensible way to overcome this problem would be to feed some grass hay along with the alfalfa and/or to include a source of inorganic phosphorus in the grain ration.

Calcium & Phosphorus Requirements

Following are some guidelines for the dietary calcium and phosphorus requirements for different classes of the horse. They should be used as rules of thumb, not as proclamations carved in granite. As pointed out above, there are many factors that would invoke a necessity to feed more or less calcium and phosphorus. These amounts were calculated assuming a horse of 1100 pounds mature weight.

Daily Needs of Calcium & Phosphorus (Adult Weight 1100 lbs)	Calcium	Phosphorus
Maintenance Horse	22 g.	14 g.
Pregnant Mare -1st & 2nd trimester	22 g.	14 g.
Pregnant Mare -3rd trimester	38 g.	28 g.
Lactating Mare	56 g.	36 g.
Nursing foal, 3 months	33 g.	18 g.
Weanling, 6 months	31 g.	16 g.
Yearling, 12 months	32 g.	17 g.
Yearling, 18 months	27 g.	15 g.
Two-year old	24 g.	13 g.
Two-year old, in training	34 g.	19 g.
Lightly Working Horse	25 g.	18 g.
Moderately Working Horse	30 g.	21 g.
Intensely Working Horse (Performance)	40 g.	29 g.
Breeding Stallion	25 g.	18 g.

How important is the calcium/phosphorus ratio?

A friend of yours has just bought a little place in Colorado. He has a few horses and says the best alfalfa hay in the world is grown there. He feeds it to all of his horses, including the young ones. They eat up to 18 pounds per day, plus he gives each of them a couple of pounds of oats. Then one day he calls to tell you that all of his youngsters' legs are swollen and puffy in the knees and fetlock joints. They can hardly walk. What should he do?

You do a few calculations and estimate that he is feeding 102 grams of calcium to 21 grams of phosphorus, nearly a 5.1 ratio, which is unacceptable for his young horses. You tell him to find some grass hay to mix with his alfalfa, to lower the total hay intake and make up the difference with more grain. And finally you tell him to add 2 ounces of monosodium phosphate to the diet.

Since you were shooting from the hip, you really didn't take the time to refigure his diet. So as you set down the phone, you put a pencil to it and come up with the following results:

Feed	Amount Fed	Calcium	Phosphorus
Alfalfa Hay	8.0 lbs.	45.0 g.	8.0 g.
Timothy Grass Hay	8.0 lbs.	15.0 g.	7.0 g.
Oats	4.0 lbs.	1.5 g.	6.0 g.
Monosodium phosphate	0.22 lbs.	0.0 g.	12.5 g.
TOTALS	**20.22 lbs.**	**61.5 g.**	**33.5 g.**

Not bad: the ratio is now down below 2:1, and even though your friend is still feeding large amounts of calcium, he now has enough phosphorus to balance it. A month later he calls to say you are a genius. All of his young horses are normal now, and running around like so many banshees. You say that you knew they would be, and you thank him for following your advice, as you pat yourself on the back.

As hard as it may be to believe, this little drama is played all too frequently, and often with far less satisfying results. Many horses are destroyed each year as a result of unwise feeding programs; horses that could be living long and healthy lives if just a few corrections were made to their diets in a timely fashion.

Magnesium (Mg)

A horse's body contains about .05% magnesium, of which 60% is found in the skeleton and teeth. This means that the body of the average horse has a little more than ½ pound of magnesium in its tissues. Obviously magnesium is a major player in the chemistry of life, yet it's a nutrient we usually do not hear too much about, for the simple reason that most grains and forages have enough magnesium to supply the needs of most horses. Magnesium is contained in the chlorophyll of green plants, a fact that ensures a fairly even distribution in the natural elements of a horse's diet. Typically, this is between 0.1% – 0.3% of dry matter.

The NRC requirement for horses ranges from about 7.5 grams per day for a maintenance horse, to 15.1 grams per day for a horse in heavy training. If we use the lower figure (0.1%) for the amount of magnesium found in natural feed, we see that enough magnesium—a little over 8 grams—is present in the diet of a maintenance horse eating 18 to 20 pounds of dry matter per day. A horse in heavy training, however, that is eating 25 to 30 pounds of dry matter per day will only obtain about 12 or 13 grams of magnesium. Such feeds include corn, and bromegrass, timothy, and orchardgrass hays. Oats and barley have a little more magnesium, with an average analysis showing concentrations of 0.16% and 0.14%, respectively. And, as you might imagine, alfalfa hay tops the list of common feeds, with 0.30% – 0.35% magnesium. A performance horse, therefore, that is receiving 10 pounds of alfalfa hay and 6 pounds each of oats and corn should be getting enough magnesium (about 24 grams). But if we substitute the alfalfa with a grass hay, the magnesium total is only around 14 grams; a little low.

In the body, magnesium is needed for the synthesis of proteins and the digestion of starches. It is also an activator for over 300 enzyme reactions. Deficiencies of magnesium can cause nervousness and muscle tremors, and eventually mineralization in the arteries and damaged capillaries. A horse receiving low levels of dietary magnesium will have a rough, lusterless haircoat. A horse receiving adequate magnesium will require less energy to perform the same amount of work as a horse receiving sub-optimal levels of this ubiquitous mineral.

Magnesium in the feed is absorbed at a rate of 40% – 60%. Inorganic forms of magnesium, such as magnesium sulfate, magnesium carbonate and magnesium oxide, are generally 70% absorbed by the horse. However, several factors can limit magnesium absorption, including high levels of calcium or phosphorus in the diet; an excess of vitamin D; diuretics, such as Lasix; and a lack of dietary protein.

Many horses that are getting what should be adequate amounts of magnesium in the diet do, in fact, display symptoms of low magnesium, such as muscle tremors, or intolerance to work or exercise. Excess calcium is the most likely cause of a magnesium deficiency, and alfalfa hay is usually the culprit. Since the absorption of both calcium and magnesium

Excess calcium is the most likely cause of a magnesium deficiency (often seen in muscle tremors or intolerance to work or exercise), and alfalfa hay is usually the culprit.

are regulated by the same hormone, an overabundance of either mineral will shut down the pipeline for both. This can lead to problems.

Obesity in many horses has been traced to inadequate levels of magnesium. The problem is known as insulin resistance, and is similar to Type II diabetes in people.

Obesity in many horses has been traced to inadequate levels of magnesium. The problem is known as insulin resistance, and is similar to Type II diabetes in people. Here's how it works: when blood sugar rises after a meal, the pancreas releases insulin to carry all this extra sugar into the body's cells, where it can then be used as fuel. The cells don't just light a fire under the sugar molecules, of course. That would be cheating. Instead, the sugar is converted into energy through a series of mind-numbingly complex enzyme reactions. Reactions that require magnesium. So, if there is too little magnesium available, the cells can't extract energy from blood sugar, the pancreas gets frustrated, and the excess blood sugar is turned into fat, fat that often appears in hard lumps along the crest of the neck, and the base of the tail.

To make matters worse, chronically high levels of insulin in the blood can lead to blockages in small blood vessels, such as those supplying blood to the feet. This, in turn, can lead to laminitis, a word every horse owner utters in hushed tones.

The good news is that most horses with problems caused by too little magnesium respond to the introduction of supplemental magnesium to the feed, and/or cutting back the amount of calcium in the diet. Magnesium carbonate and magnesium oxide are cheap, readily available, and well utilized by the horse. However, since organic (chelated or proteinated) magnesium can be absorbed through different pathways, it will work better for you if you're having a problem cutting back the calcium (if you have a barn full of high-calcium alfalfa hay). For problem horses, a good calcium to magnesium ratio to strive for is 1½:1 to 2:1.

Sulfur (S)

The depth of the controversy surrounding the mineral sulfur is exceeded only by our lack of knowledge about just what sulfur does in the body. In this section known facts about sulfur are presented; controversy is reserved for the section on MSM in Chapter 10, "Exotic Nutrients."

Sulfur accounts for about 0.15% of a horse's mass. The body of the average horse, then, contains a little more than 1½ pounds of sulfur. Most of this is contained in the hooves and the hair, which are both around 3% sulfur. There are two amino acids that contain sulfur: methionine and cystine. Methionine is an essential amino acid that must be present in the diet. Cystine is not considered to be an essential amino acid, as long as there is plenty of methionine, since the body can easily synthesize the former from the latter. (Except for the addition of one sulfur atom and one hydrogen atom, cystine is identical to the major portion of the methionine molecule.)

In addition, sulfur is present in the vitamins biotin and thiamin (B_1), insulin (which regulates blood sugar), heparin (an anticoagulant), and chondroitin sulfate, a major constituent of joint and connective tissue.

Sulfur gets around. By going through the list of nutrients that contain sulfur, we can see that without it a horse would be in quite a fix. It could not metabolize carbohydrates or even simple blood sugar. Hooves and hair could not grow, blood could not flow, and joints would not move. Not that any of this makes much difference, because without sulfur a horse would literally fall apart at the seams, since it is the disulfide bond in cystine that gives protein its shape.

Yet I cannot tell you just how much sulfur a horse needs, because no one really knows a horse's sulfur requirement. We do know that a good quality protein source will contain about 0.15% sulfur, and this appears to be enough for most horses. Many veterinarians and farriers suggest supplementation of methionine and biotin for horses with foot and hoof problems, and in many cases this is sound advice, although if the goal is simply to provide your horse with more sulfur, methionine is far and away the cheaper of the two. In olden times, raw sulfur was fed as a means to improve and maintain hoof quality, and to some extent this practice is used today. Elemental sulfur, however, is not a natural nutrient, and its liberal use should be cautioned against.

How much sulfur is too much? Again, it's hard to say, but certainly more than the prudent horseman is likely to feed. It is known that excess sulfur can inhibit copper absorption in ruminants, but this has not been seen in horses.

Potassium (K)

Potassium is an important mineral in the regulation of osmotic pressure, and the acid-base balance within the body. Osmotic pressure is controlled by potassium and sodium working together to regulate the fluid content within the cells of the body. Potassium also plays a role in the transmission of nerve impulses, and in proper muscle function. Many horses suffering from Azoturia (tying up) have been found to have low levels of potassium, calcium and/or sodium, and have responded favorably to the introduction of higher levels of these minerals into the diet. Horses deficient in potassium will lose their appetites, and eventually refuse to eat. Weight loss and a generally poor appearance can be the result of a diet low in potassium.

Forages are relatively high in potassium, while cereal grains are lacking. Alfalfa hay on the average will be around 1.40% potassium. Grass hays will range from 1.60% – 2.90%, with orchardgrass topping the list. Oats, corn and barley all fall between 0.30% – 0.45%.

Horses deficient in potassium will lose their appetites, and eventually refuse to eat.

The potassium requirements of different classes of adult horses range from about 25 grams per day for an 1100 pound maintenance horse, to 50 grams per day for a horse in heavy training. Lactating mares need nearly as much as horses in heavy training (around 46 grams), while a mare in the last month of pregnancy will only need 31 grams per day. The amount of potassium needed by young horses (with an estimated adult weight of 1100 pounds) ranges from 13 grams per day for a 6-month-old weanling, to 21 grams per day for an 18-month-old horse in training.

Horses whose diets consist primarily of hay or pasture should not need any additional potassium. A horse eating 14 pounds of average hay, for example, would be getting over 95 grams of potassium. On the other hand, horses on high grain diets and/or horses that sweat profusely, such as race horses or endurance horses, probably should be given extra potassium. Potassium chloride is very inexpensive and can be readily added as a top dressing on the feed. There are also several good electrolyte formulas on the market that contain potassium. They can either be added to the feed, or dissolved in water.

Salt (Sodium Chloride – NaCl)

No matter what you are feeding, it's very doubtful that it contains enough salt, unless it was added at the feed mill. Grains and forages do not provide enough sodium or chloride to maintain most horses, so it should **always** be offered free choice, either loose or in a block, and always with abundant water nearby. Salt blocks can be straight salt, iodized salt, or mineralized salt that contains many important trace minerals.

Horses not getting enough salt will eat slower than normal, and will drink less water. Often they will develop the habit of licking, especially things that have dried sweat on them, such as shovel handles.

Sodium and chloride help maintain the acid-base balance within the body, and assist in the osmotic regulation of body fluids. Sodium acts in concert with potassium to regulate the fluid content of cells; potassium keeps the cells from drying out, while sodium keeps them from filling with water.

Horses not getting enough salt will eat slower than normal, and will drink less water. They will develop rough haircoats and dry skin. Often they will develop the habit of licking, especially things that have dried sweat on them, such as shovel handles.

Since so much salt is lost in sweat, the requirement for it increases in proportion to the amount of work a horse is doing. While a maintenance horse might get by with 8 or 9 grams of sodium per day and a lactating mare will only need 10 to 12 grams, a horse in heavy training will require 35 to 40 grams per day. For horses in training, loose salt is preferable to a block. It takes 102 grams of salt to supply 40 grams of sodium, and that makes for a lot of licking!

Quick Summary of Macrominerals

- **Calcium** is plentiful in hay, especially alfalfa hay.
- Alfalfa hays often have Ca to P ratios of 5:1 or 6:1, but can be as high as 8:1.
- Cereal grains have more **phosphorus** than **calcium**.
- It is much easier to feed too much calcium, than too much **phosphorus**.
- **Calcium** is absorbed with 55% – 70% efficiency.
- **Phosphorus** is absorbed with 30% – 55% efficiency.
- **Calcium** and **phosphorus** are more easily absorbed from inorganic sources.
- The maximum tolerable **calcium** to **phosphorus** ratio for mature horses is 5:1; for growing horses, 3:1. The optimum ratio is between 1:1 and 2:1.
- An excess of **calcium** can interfere with **magnesium** absorption.
- A prolonged deficiency of **magnesium** can lead to obesity, insulin-intolerance, and laminitis.
- **Magnesium** is needed for protein synthesis, starch digestion, and the functioning of enzymes.
- Grains and forages usually contain enough **magnesium** for most horses.
- **Sulfur** is needed for sugar and carbohydrate metabolism, and it is present in many key compounds in the body.
- No dietary minimum requirement has been established for **sulfur**, although its importance in the body is well recognized.
- The amino acid, methionine, is the most common source of dietary **sulfur**.
- Horses are tolerant of large amounts of **sulfur**.
- Forages are high in **potassium**; cereal grains are low.
- **Sodium** is lacking in most common feeds.
- **Potassium** and **salt** are lost in sweat, increasing the requirement in working horses.
- **Potassium** chloride is inexpensive and can easily be added to the grain.
- **Salt** should always be offered free choice, with plenty of water.

TRACE MINERALS

1948

"For many years the importance of common salt and of phosphorus and calcium in livestock feeding has been recognized. Only recently, however, have experiments revealed the need in some areas of supplying stock with certain 'trace elements,' such as iodine, cobalt and copper."   FRANK B. MORRISON, *FEEDS AND FEEDING: 21ST EDITION*, 1948

Trace minerals are essential for life, but needed in smaller quantities than the macrominerals. They are all further down on the periodic table than the macrominerals, which means they are heavier and generally less abundant in nature than their more prevalent cousins.

Another curious difference is that most trace minerals are absorbed better when they are part of an organic substrate, while the macrominerals are better absorbed in inorganic form. Sodium chloride, potassium chloride, magnesium oxide, monosodium phosphate, dicalcium phosphate—all of these inorganic compounds deliver minerals more efficiently to the body than their organic counterparts (though I may get some dissenting opinions in the case of magnesium). The exception is sulfur, which is virtually unavailable to the body when supplied inorganically. Of the seven trace minerals under discussion here, (cobalt, copper, iodine, iron, manganese, selenium and zinc) only one, selenium, is better absorbed in inorganic forms.

Another curious difference is that most trace minerals are absorbed better when they are part of an organic substrate, while macrominerals are better absorbed in inorganic form.

Trace minerals are vitally important to the health of your horse. The fact that they are needed in such small quantities should not undermine their essential metabolic roles. The important thing to remember is that nature always builds with the materials she has at hand. It is no coincidence that the energy supplying nutrients—carbohydrates, fats and proteins—are all composed of atmospheric gases, and neither is it coincidence that trace minerals have been incorporated into the process of life in amounts commensurate with their abundance in the soil.

But what if soils—namely farmland—were to slowly become depleted of certain elements necessary to sustain life? It would be quite a deleterious development for the animals (ourselves included) that depend on farm produce to remain strong and healthy. Unfortunately, this is happening now, and has been happening for several decades.

In the past, before urbanization and the widespread distribution of farm products, all minerals brought up from the soil by grasses, trees, and other vegetation, were returned to it. The soil was nourished by the wastes and the bodies of animals that lived and died upon it. But times have changed. Today, Colorado beef grown on Iowa corn is shipped to South America. Much of Nebraska's wheat ends up on a slow boat to Russia. North Dakota oats nourish horses between Florida and California. As all of these products leave the areas where they were produced, the minerals they contain go with them—on a one-way ticket.

Additionally, midwestern and southern farmland receiving high levels of rainfall each year is subject to leaching of trace minerals. (Leaching is the loss of nutrients by water washing them from the soil.) Irrigated fields undergo similar losses. Over many years, these elements are lost, causing forages and grains to be deficient in these important nutrients.

Farmers fertilize with nitrogen, phosphorus and potassium, and occasionally calcium, but that leaves 18 to 20 minerals essential to horses (and horsemen) that are not being returned to the ground. Since plants don't require the high levels of minerals that animals need in order to thrive, even perfectly healthy-looking grains and forages often cannot supply the levels of minerals our horses require.

The demineralization of our soil is not the slow process we might imagine. Tests done on dehydrated alfalfa meal by the National Academy of Sciences between 1973 and 1981 yielded some disturbing results. Copper dropped from 11.2 PPM to 9.5 PPM during that period; iron went from 330 PPM to 270 PPM; zinc fell from 21.5 PPM to 19.4 PPM. These figures represent losses of 15%, 18% and 10%, respectively, in less than a decade.

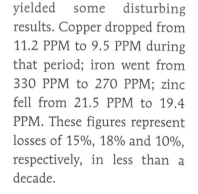

The demineralization of our soil is not the slow process we might imagine. Tests done on dehydrated alfalfa meal between 1973 and 1981 yielded some disturbing results.

Organic vs. Inorganic Trace Minerals

The depletion of our soils is a phenomenon well-known to the feed industry. Most feed and supplement manufacturers fortify their products with minerals. Every year, millions of tons of ground ores, in the forms of oxides, sulfates, and carbonates, are processed and added to feed, food, and supplements for domestic animals and humans. But how good are they?

As we have already seen, inorganic macrominerals are generally quite efficient, even better than organic forms in most cases. But inorganic trace minerals are not nearly as well absorbed. Once a trace mineral becomes disassociated from the salt (sulfate, carbonate, etc.) it was bound to, it takes on a positive charge, which binds it like a magnet to the negatively charged intestinal wall, thus denying it passage into the cells.

Organic minerals, in contrast to inorganic sulfate, oxide and carbonate forms, are either electrically neutral, or have only a slight negative charge. This neutrality is the primary reason organic trace minerals are better absorbed. There are two general categories of organic minerals: complexes, and chelates and proteinates.

Complexes

Complexes can be either in polysaccharide or amino acid form. In polysaccharide complexes, the mineral is encapsulated, or "sequestered" in a coating of giant sea kelp. Polysaccharide complexes are not organic in the true sense of the word, since the mineral (usually in sulfate form) is not chemically bound to the polysaccharide substrate. They owe their effectiveness to the fact that the complex is largely protected from the digestive process until it reaches the intestine, where the substrate dissolves and the mineral can then undergo a natural chelation process that increases its chance of absorbtion. Amino acid complexes tend to be a little more stable than the polysaccharide forms. Otherwise they react similarly to improve trace mineral bio-availability. One major advantage of complexes over simple inorganic sulfates is the fact that they do not usually react with fragile vitamins in feeds and supplements. This can greatly improve vitamin stability in such products.

Chelates and Proteinates

In contrast to complexes, chelates and proteinates are chemically bound, through a commercial process, to specific amino acid or protein digest fragments, before they ever get into your horse's feed. The term chelate (pronounced KEY-late) is derived from the Latin word "chelae," which literally means "scorpion claws." The analogy is an apt one if we imagine a scorpion holding a BB between the tips of its claws. Chemically, a chelate is a five or six-sided ring containing a positively-charged metal ion. The metal ion is held fast within the ring by negatively charged electrons. A true chelate will have two or more points of attachment to the metal ion, which improves the stability.

The difference between chelated and proteinated minerals is subtle. By definition, a chelate is an entity in which the metal ion is chemically bound to a known combination of amino acids, whereas a proteinate is a chelate consisting of amino acids or partially hydrolyzed protein. Proteinates are more difficult to manufacture properly, cost more to produce, but may be more effective than straight chelates.

Feeding Organic Minerals

The manufacturers of polysaccharide complexes recommend that they be fed just as though they were regular sulfates, oxides and carbonates. While they are considerably more efficient than regular inorganic trace minerals, they are not bullet-proof, and they do allow the horse's body some degree of discretion over what to absorb, and what not to.

On the other hand, chelates—and especially proteinates—are extremely effective organic entities that are so well absorbed that a serious mineral imbalance could result from their misuse. For that reason, the manufacturers recommend that chelates and proteinates should only comprise 20% – 33% of the total trace mineral content added to the feed, the difference being made up with inorganic minerals.

Since trace minerals are so important, serious horsemen should consider adding organic trace minerals to their horses' rations, if extra minerals are needed. Performance and breeding horses are especially responsive to the addition of organic trace minerals to their diets.

Organic Forms
• Polysaccharide Complex
• Amino Acid Complex
• Chelate
• Proteinate
Inorganic Forms
• Sulfate
• Chloride
• Oxide
• Carbonate
• Phosphate

The Trace Elements

Cobalt (Co)

The mineral cobalt is necessary for the synthesis of vitamin B_{12}, which in turn is needed for the formation of hemoglobin.

This is the solitary known function of cobalt. The minimum requirements for cobalt have not been thoroughly studied, but a range from 0.8 milligrams (mg.) per day for a maintenance horse to 1.1 mg. per day for a performance horse are considered adequate. A cobalt deficiency can cause anemia, reduced appetite, and a slowed rate of growth.

Forages generally contain 0.09 – 0.16 mg./lb. of cobalt, while grains have between 0.025 – 0.22 mg./lb., though these amounts can vary from place to place. A horse eating 14 pounds of feed with an average cobalt content of 0.10 mg./lb. would, therefore, be getting enough. Cobalt is usually included in small quantities in mineral blocks and supplements.

A cobalt deficiency can cause anemia, reduced appetite, and a slowed rate of growth.

Copper (Cu)

The horse's body puts copper to work in a number of places. It is needed for many of the enzyme systems involved in the manufacture and maintenance of connective tissue, utilization of iron, maintenance of mitochondria within the cell nucleus, and the synthesis of the pigment melanin. Copper is also required for bone formation, maintaining the elastic strength of blood vessels, the manufacture of hemoglobin, and the healing of wounds. Copper is especially important for maintaining an efficient immune system.

Like all minerals, copper must be in a proper balance with other macro and microminerals. A deficiency of copper can result from a diet too high in calcium, iron, molybdenum and zinc, and also by a diet low in protein. A horse fed a copper deficient diet—or a diet high in copper limiting nutrients—may develop enlarged joints and fragile bones. Its growth will be slowed and it may become anemic. Osteochondrosis, or metabolic bone disease, may result from a prolonged copper deficiency.

The minimum requirements for dietary copper range from 82 milligrams per day for the maintenance horse, to 115 milligrams per day for a performance horse, though optimum amounts may be somewhat higher. Horses can tolerate much higher levels of copper than the minimum requirement.

Forages usually contain between 4 - 11 mg./lb. of copper, but the availability of copper in forages is only in the 6% - 34% range. Grass hays are generally higher in copper than alfalfa hay. Grains have less copper than forages, with amounts ranging from 1.6 mg./lb. for corn to 3.7 mg./lb. for barley. Most feed, therefore, does not contain enough copper for most horses—especially horses on high carbohydrate diets—and some degree of supplementation would be beneficial.

Iodine (I)

Most of us have never seen a person or animal with a goiter—a condition in which the thyroid gland becomes so swollen that a large, unsightly protrusion develops on the neck—and we have iodized salt to thank for that fact. Goiters were common in people, livestock and pets until the early 1900s, when it was discovered that dietary iodine would cure goiters and reverse other symptoms of low thyroid activity. (The first test to determine if supplemental iodine would cure goiters was conducted in Cleveland in 1916.)

The thyroid gland, which is responsible for regulating the rate of metabolism, produces two amino acid-like hormones (thyroxine and triiodothyronine) that both contain iodine. When there is too little iodine in the diet, the gland is stimulated by a different hormone that causes it to swell. Thyroid hormones can be thought of as metronomes for the body. They determine the rate at which the body consumes oxygen, burns glucose, and synthesizes protein.

Though mature horses seldom develop goiters, they are common in foals born to iodine-deficient mares. Such foals will have trouble standing to nurse, and will appear to be very weak. Mares that are deficient in iodine may have abnormal estrous cycles. Other symptoms include rough haircoats, brittle hooves and sparse hair.

> Though mature horses seldom develop goiters, they are common in foals born to iodine-deficient mares. Such foals will have trouble standing to nurse, and will appear to be very weak.

The minimum iodine requirement is estimated at 0.1 PPM in the diet. Some common feedstuffs can contain as much as 2 PPM iodine, while others contain none, at all, depending on where they were grown. Many areas of the United States have iodine-deficient soil, particularly in the Great Lakes Basin, as well as a number of midwestern, western, and northern states. But there is no need to have your feed tested for iodine, since iodized salt—salt that contains 70 PPM of iodine—is available for the same price as the regular salt you should already be giving your horse free-choice.

Iron (Fe)

Most of what iron does in the body is related to the transport of oxygen to the cells, which means there is little that goes on in the body that does not involve iron. Its most notable presence is in the hemoglobin molecule, the primary constituent of the red blood cell where, in the average horse, 60% of the body's 33 grams of iron can be found. It is also a component of myoglobin, a hemoglobin-like compound that loosely holds oxygen in the muscles when it's abundant, and releases it when the body needs it.

Iron is a mineral the horseman needs to be careful with. There are probably more problems caused by an over-abundance of iron, than by a lack of it. Even though the absorption rate is low (between 10% – 15%), grains and for-ages generally contain enough iron for the needs of most horses. Exceptions would include horses under stress; horses that have lost a lot of blood from injuries; and horses stressed by heavy parasitic loads. High levels of cadmium, cobalt, cop-per, zinc and manganese can also limit iron absorption.

The minimum iron requirement for a maintenance horse is 40 PPM, or about 18.14 milligrams in each pound of feed. Growing foals, late pregnant and lactating mares should have more on the order of 50 PPM in the entire ration, which works out to about 22.68 milligrams per pound of feed. Most common feeds contain at least 65 PPM, with a few exceptions, such as corn and timothy hay, which usually contain less than 40 PPM. Alfalfa hay, on the other hand, often contains more than 200 PPM of iron. Since iron is so well conserved in the body, iron supplementation should not be necessary for most horses, though the judi-cious addition of iron to the diets of young, fast growing horses, lactating or pregnant mares, and performance horses can be beneficial.

Myths about iron are

Iron is a mineral the horseman needs to be careful with. There are probably more problems caused by an overabundance of iron, than by a lack of it.

rife in the performance horse community. It is a belief held by some race horse trainers that feeding outrageous amounts of iron—or worse, injecting it—will enhance the production of red blood cells, which in turn will increase the packed cell volume and augment the blood's capacity for carrying oxygen. Often the outcome is the opposite of the desired effect: a tired, fatigued horse that can't seem to keep weight on.

High levels of iron will lower the amount of available zinc and copper, which in turn can lead to other mineral imbalances. It can adversely affect the metabolism of phosphorus, which can result in a slowed rate of growth accompanied by poorly mineralized bone. Also, many pathogenic bacteria have a high requirement for iron. Thus, excess iron may make bacterial infections worse.

Most popular liquid "iron tonics" contain a daily dose of 450 to 550 milligrams of iron—more than the daily iron requirement for most horses—in widely varying forms. The better ones also include balanced amounts of other important trace minerals along with a full spectrum of vitamins. Many successful trainers swear by these products, and some of the better products certainly can be beneficial to high-powered horses under a lot of stress. On the other hand, there are a few "jug" products that are not worth the cost of the bottle they come in. As with most everything, you get what you pay for.

Manganese (Mn)

Not much attention was given to manganese by horsemen until recently, when glucosamine and chondroitin sulfate supplements became so popular. Chondroitin sulfate is one of the main constituents of joint cartilage, and manganese is required by the enzymes that facilitate its utilization.

Manganese is also needed for carbohydrate and fat metabolism, and for normal reproductive function.

Little work has been done to establish the manganese requirement for horses, but it's generally believed that 40 PPM in the diet is adequate. Timothy hay and orchardgrass hay both contain more than that—50 PPM and 140 PPM respectively—but most other common feeds are lacking. Alfalfa hay contains around 25 PPM manganese (and lower amounts when the calcium level is high), oats have around 36 PPM, barley 16 PPM, and corn bottoms-out the list with only 5 PPM. Some degree of supplementation, therefore, should be a consideration, especially for growing horses and performance horses.

Since manganese is so vitally important for the formation of connective tissues, foals born to mares deficient in manganese may have crooked legs and deformed joints with severely limited articulation. Performance horses not receiving enough manganese will exhibit stiff joints and general soreness, and will not want to work.

Just as the minimum requirements for this mineral are not fully known, neither is the level of toxicity, but an excess in the diet could be expected to interfere with the absorption and utilization of other nutrients.

Zinc (Zn)

Zinc is another mineral that really gets around. It is found in high concentrations in the eye and the prostate gland, as well as in the skin, hair and hooves. It's essential for

Typical Zinc Content of Common Forages and Grains	
Alfalfa Hay	28 PPM
Barley	17 PPM
Bromegrass Hay	26 PPM
Corn	19 PPM
Oats	35 PPM
Orchardgrass Hay	36 PPM
Timothy Hay	38 PPM

Adequate amounts of zinc are lacking in almost every common grain and forage. Interestingly, zinc deficiency is not a widespread problem, probably because most feed mills include some form of supplemental zinc in their grain rations.

as many as 340 enzyme systems, a fact which greatly underscores its importance in the body. Among the many functions of zinc, it is needed for skin growth and healing, normal prostate function, and phosphorus and protein metabolism.

Adequate amounts of zinc are lacking in almost every common grain and forage. Although the minimum requirement for zinc is believed to be between 40 – 50 PPM in the total diet, the optimum range is probably closer to 90 PPM. But most common feeds contain levels below 40 PPM.

Interestingly, zinc deficiency is not a widespread problem, probably because most feed mills include some form of supplemental zinc in their grain rations. Inorganic sources of supplemental zinc include zinc oxide and zinc sulfate, of which zinc sulfate is the most easily absorbed by the horse. Zinc is also available in polysaccharide and amino acid complexes, amino acid chelates, and proteinates.

The absorption rate of zinc is in the 10% – 15% range, and this rate can vary, according to how much zinc is already in the body, and the form in which zinc is supplied. Foals deficient in zinc will have poor appetites, a reduced rate of growth, hair loss, and dry, scaly skin.

Zinc is also needed for growth and maintenance of the hoof wall, and for that reason it's widely used in hoof supplements, often in the form of zinc-methionine complex. These supplements vary widely in their formulations, but the efficacy of some of the better ones cannot be denied.

High levels of zinc are well tolerated by horses, although too much of it can interfere with the utilization of other minerals, especially copper.

Selenium (Se)

In the case of selenium, if a little is good, a lot is definitely not better. In fact, selenium is so toxic that, until the late 1970's, selenium could not legally be added to feed. Fortunately for horsemen, the FDA now permits the addition of selenium to horse feeds, a fact which makes life much easier for those living in areas with selenium-deficient soils.

Along with vitamin E (a vitamin that works synergistically with selenium), selenium is needed for proper muscle development. It is a component of the enzymes that detoxify the peroxides so destructive to cell membranes.

The maintenance requirement for selenium is estimated to be 0.1 PPM in the diet, while the maximum tolerable amount is 2 PPM in the total diet, or 20 times the maintenance requirement. Most feedstuffs contain between 0.05 – 0.3 PPM, though levels vary greatly, depending upon the nature of the soil. Areas low in selenium include the Great Lakes states, New England, Florida, northern California, western Oregon and western and northern Washington state. States that have localized areas with toxic levels of selenium include the band of states stretching from northern New Mexico and Texas through Montana and North Dakota.

A selenium deficiency in

In the case of selenium, if a little is good a lot is definitely not better. In fact, selenium is so toxic that, until the late 1970's, selenium could not legally be added to feed.

the foal manifests itself as white muscle disease, a form of muscular dystrophy, so called because the animal becomes pale in appearance. Symptoms include general weakness and labored movement, difficulty in nursing and swallowing, and irregular, labored breathing.

Acute selenium toxicity is sometimes called blind staggers, or simply alkali disease. Affected horses appear colicky with an elevated heart rate and irregular breathing, and may appear to be blind. They can be seen pressing their heads against stationary objects, and may sweat profusely. These symptoms can be triggered by the ingestion of 150 milligrams per 100 lbs. of body weight, or 1.66 grams for an 1100 pound horse.

Symptoms of chronic toxicity include anemia, lameness and joint stiffness, a rough hair coat with loss of hair in the mane and tail, and malformed hooves with cracks around the coronary band. If these symptoms go unchecked for a long period of time, chronic toxicity can cause death.

Selenium is easily absorbed by the body of the horse, with an efficiency rate above 75%. In nature, selenium forms complexes with the amino acids cystine, cysteine, and methionine. Sodium selenite and sodium selenate are the usual supplemental forms.

Your goal in supplementing selenium should be to bring the selenium concentration in the entire ration to 0.1 PPM. Before supplementing, therefore, you should know how much you are already feeding. If you know where your hay was grown, a quick call to your county extension agent should be helpful in determining if it was grown in a selenium deficient area, or not. If in doubt have your hay tested; selenium is serious business.

Chart of Daily Mineral Requirements

Based on 1100 lb. Adult Weight

	Calcium (g.)	Phosphorous (g.)	Magnesium (g.)	Sulfur (g.)	Potassium (g.)	Sodium** (g.)	Cobalt* (g.)	Copper (mg.)	Iodine (mg.)	Iron (mg.)	Manganese* (mg.)	Zinc (mg.)	Selenium (mg.)
Pregnant Mare, Early to Mid	22	14	8.0	12.3	25	8.2	0.8	82	0.8	327	327	327	0.8
Pregnant Mare, 3rd Trimester	38	28	9.4	12.3	31	8.2	0.8	82	0.8	409	327	327	0.8
Lactating Mare	56	36	10.9	16.3	46	10.9	1.1	108	1.1	543	424	434	1.1
Foal at 3 months	33	18	3.5	6.5	10	4.4	0.4	44	0.4	218	174	174	0.4
Weanling at 6 months	31	16	4.1	7.9	13	5.3	0.5	53	0.5	265	212	212	0.5
Yearling at 12 months	32	17	6.0	10.7	18	7.1	0.7	71	0.7	356	285	285	0.7
Yearling at 18 months	27	15	6.5	11.9	21	7.9	0.8	80	0.8	396	317	317	0.8
2-year-old in Training	34	19	10.0	14.8	32	9.9	1.0	99	1.0	495	396	396	1.0
Maintenance Horse	22	14	3.0	12.3	25	8.2	0.8	82	0.8	327	327	327	0.8
Performance Horse in Training	40	29	15.1	17.2	50	34.5	1.1	115	1.1	459	459	459	1.1
Breeding Stallion	25	18	9.4	12.8	31	8.5	0.9	86	0.9	341	341	341	0.9

* There is no minimum requirement established for this mineral. The quantities shown are based on NRC estimates for safe and adequate amounts.

** Salt is 39% Sodium.

Quick Summary of Trace Minerals

- **Trace minerals** are less abundant in soil than macrominerals.
- **Trace minerals** are diminishing from the soil, due mainly to the effects of farming.
- Organic forms of **copper, cobalt, iodine, iron, manganese** and **zinc** are absorbed better than inorganic forms.
- **Polysaccharide complexes** are sulfates enclosed in a polysaccharide coating.
- **Chelates** and **proteinates** are chemically bound to organic substrates, and are very effective.
- **Cobalt** is the central atom in the vitamin B_{12} molecule, which is needed for the formation of hemoglobin.
- **Copper** is part of several enzyme systems that maintain and synthesize connective tissue, aid in reproduction, and promote an active immune system.
- **Iodine** is used in the manufacture of thyroid hormones. A deficiency can cause goiters in young animals. Iodized salt will provide a horse with sufficient iodine.
- **Iron** is a constituent of hemoglobin and myoglobin, which transport and store oxygen in the blood and muscles.
- **Manganese** is needed by the enzymes that regulate the manufacture and utilization of chondroitin sulfates, important compounds in connective tissues.
- **Zinc** is part of several enzyme systems necessary for the growth and maintenance of hooves, hair and skin. It is lacking in almost every common feed.
- **Selenium** is needed for proper muscle growth and function. Soils in many areas of the U.S. are deficient, others contain toxic levels.

CHAPTER 9

Vitamins:
The Missing Puzzle Pieces

1948

"One of the exceedingly important facts in livestock production is that all green forage crops are rich in nearly all the vitamins required by farm animals."

FRANK B. MORRISON, *FEEDS AND FEEDING, 21ST EDITION, 1948*

*E*very nutrient we have looked at so far has had some compelling chemical characteristic that makes it easy to identify as a member of a specific group: carbohydrates contain hydrogen and oxygen in the same ratio as water; fats are all soluble in ether; proteins are made up of distinct amino acids, and minerals are simply individual elements put to work within the body as constituents of enzymes or other important compounds.

But vitamins have no distinctive chemical signature; some are readily soluble, others are not; some are alcohols, some more closely resemble proteins; some can take great extremes of heat, others fall apart at the slightest provocation; most, but not all, act as coenzymes, or parts of coenzymes. A chemist cannot look at a vitamin and declare it to be one, until it is proven empirically to be needed by the body.

So what is a vitamin? A vitamin is, by simple default, what is still needed by the body after it is given all the carbohydrates, fats, proteins and minerals it needs. Vitamins comprise the seemingly unlikely group of nutrients that fall through the nutritional cracks. To put it another way, if you were given a jigsaw puzzle called "The Nutritional Requirements of the Horse," and you arranged all the pieces of carbohydrates, fats, proteins, and minerals in proper order, you would see large gaps between many of the pieces. The gaps would be filled with vitamins, the missing pieces in the puzzle of nutrition.

Vitamins are classified as either fat-soluble or water-soluble, although this is not an absolute division, as some fat-soluble vita-

A vitamin is, by simple default, what is still needed by the body after it is given all the carbohydrates, fats, proteins and minerals it needs.

mins can be made to dissolve in water, and vice versa. The fat-soluble vitamins are vitamins only for vertebrates, while most of the water-soluble vitamins are needed by all animals. Most, but not all, water-soluble vitamins are present in yeast.

Fat-Soluble Vitamins

Vitamins A, D, E and K are the fat-soluble vitamins. All are guaranteed in IU (International Units) per pound, except for vitamin K which, along with the water-soluble vitamins, is guaranteed in milligrams per pound. Vitamin D_3 is sometimes guaranteed in ICU (International Chick Units), though IU is more common.

Vitamin A

The term "vitamin A" does not refer to any specific compound, but rather to a class of at least a dozen compounds that all display the same activity in the body. Moreover, plants do not manufacture vitamin A; it is only made in the bodies of animals with backbones (and in large vitamin factories, mostly in Europe). What plants **do** make is a class of pigments known as carotenoids, of which about 50 can—to varying degrees—be converted into vitamin A in the body. Of the carotenoids, the most important is beta carotene.

Vitamin A is important for vision, since it is a chief component of the light-sensitive pigment in the rods of the eye. It's also essential for cell differentiation (so bone cells become bone, and liver cells become liver), and to assist in the continuing process of bone remodeling in growing horses.

The list of symptoms that point toward a deficiency include: poor growth and depressed appetite; progressive weakness; impaired reproductive function; continuously

A horse on green pasture will get all the vitamin A it needs, precluding the need for any supplementation; fresh, green pasture contains 10 to 120 times more active vitamin A-precursors than dried hay.

runny, teary eyes; night blindness; a hardening of the skin and the cornea of the eyes; respiratory infections, and abscesses of the salivary glands.

The NRC estimates the bare requirement for vitamin A to be 30 – 60 IU (International Units) per day, for each kilogram of body weight. For an 1100 pound horse this would translate to 15,000 – 30,000 IU per day. At the other end of the spectrum, the upper limit set by the NRC for vitamin A on a continual basis is 16,000 IU per kilogram of dry feed, which would be 160,000 IU for a horse weighing 1100 pounds and eating 22 pounds of dry matter per day. A safe bet would be to try for the middle ground—somewhere between 60,000 – 100,000 IU per day for an 1100 pound horse.

A horse on green pasture will get all the vitamin A it needs, precluding the need for any supplementation. Sunlight, moisture and time, however, are anathema to beta carotene—fresh, green pasture contains 10 to 120 times more active vitamin A-precursors than dried hay. And cereal grains, with the exception of corn, contain almost no beta carotene, so you should expect virtually all of your horse's vitamin A to come from forages and supplements.

But nature has a way of preparing for lean times. Vitamin A is stored well in the body, primarily in the liver, and beta carotene can be stored in fat cells within the body, where it can be converted into vitamin A as the need arises. Therefore, a horse taken off of green pasture and put on dried forages is a long way from developing a vitamin A deficiency.

Generally, stored hays contain less than 40 mgs./kg. of

beta carotene. Now, since it is estimated that a horse can convert one milligram of beta carotene into 400 IU of vitamin A, a horse eating 8 kilograms (17.6 pounds) of hay per day will get only 3,200 IU of vitamin A in its hay, at best, and perhaps a lot less. Fortunately, most feed mills add vitamin A to their grain mixes. The sweet feed I use has 4,000 IU per pound, so when I feed four pounds a day I am getting the bare minimum requirement for vitamin A. In the wintertime, or when I take a horse off of pasture, I also feed 2 ounces of a supplement that supplies 400,000 IU of vitamin A per pound (or 25,000 IU per ounce), which adds another 50,000 IU to the diet. This keeps an 1100 pound horse well within the comfort zone.

From Hay	3,200 IU
From Sweet Feed	16,000 IU
From Supplement	50,000 IU
Total Vitamin A	**69,200 IU**

Like almost anything else, too much vitamin A can be toxic. Signs of chronic toxicity include: abnormal thickening of the bone accompanied by bone fragility; flaky skin; poor muscle tone; rough haircoat and loss of hair; and depression. Mares fed toxic levels of vitamin A throughout their pregnancies can give birth to grotesquely disfigured foals. It's food for thought.

Many horsemen prefer to supplement with beta carotene, instead of vitamin A. Since beta carotene is the horse's natural source of vitamin A, it is hard to argue with that decision. Beta carotene is not toxic, and may have advantages over synthetic vitamin A, such as better reproductive performance in breeding stock, and antioxidant activity in performance horses. Unfortunately, it's quite expensive and not readily available in most feed and tack stores.

Vitamin D

Vitamin D is a most interesting vitamin; not because it possesses the ability to take a nag from the glue factory to the winner's circle, but because it's the only nutrient known to be more prevalent in dried forages than in green pasture. This is because vitamin D_2 is made in plant tissues from the compound ergosterol, and ultraviolet light from the sun. But since active chlorophyll blocks the UV light from the underlying ergosterol, the vitamin D is produced only after the plant has been cut.

Fortunately for those of us who pasture our horses, another form of vitamin D (vitamin D_3) is made under the horse's skin from a form of cholesterol (7-dehydrocholesterol, to be precise), when the horse is exposed to sunlight. This all works out quite well, since the only horse liable to be denied access to sunlight is a stable-bound horse being fed dried forage.

By whatever means a horse gets its vitamin D, it is critically important that it does, because without vitamin D, a life-threatening mineral imbalance will result. Vitamin D is part of the proteins that bind calcium and magnesium, facilitating their absorption. It also helps regulate the excretion of phosphates in the urine. Simply put, a vitamin D deficiency manifests itself as a deficiency of calcium, magnesium, and phosphorus. Though a deficiency of vitamin D is extremely rare, when it does occur it produces rickets-like symptoms, including poor bone density, swollen joints, and a painful, labored gait.

An excess of vitamin D will result in the deposition of calcium in the soft tissues, primarily in the blood vessels, heart, lungs and kidneys. This most likely occurs by over-feeding supplements containing vitamin D. Some plants, such as jasmine (Cestrum diurnum), contain a substance that causes hyper-absorption of calcium, and horses eating these plants can develop a condition that resembles vitamin D toxicity.

Although vitamin D supplementation is not considered necessary, especially for horses exposed to sunlight, the addition of vitamin D_3 to the feed of young growing horses, lactating mares, or mares in the final trimester of pregnancy may be helpful. The maximum safe level suggested by the NRC for feeding on a daily basis is 2,200 IU of vitamin D_3 per kilogram of dry matter in the diet. There are many supplements offered by reputable manufacturers that have safe levels of vitamin D_3.

Vitamin D is a most interesting vitamin. Vitamin D_2 is the only nutrient known that is more prevalent in dried forages than in green pasture. Fortunately for those of us who pasture our horses, another form of vitamin D (vitamin D_3) is made under the horse's skin when the horse is exposed to sunlight.

Vitamin E

Of all the nutrients, vitamin E is the most altruistic. It selflessly offers itself up for annihilation, so the body does not destroy itself. How does it do this? Well, it all has to do with oxygen, which can be very destructive at times. (I am painfully reminded of this fact every time I look at the rusted-out quarter-panels on my old Chevy pickup.) Vitamin E is easily oxidized, which is to say that it readily reacts with charged oxygen-containing compounds, thus preventing them from reacting with—and thereby destroying—fats and proteins in the cell membrane. Simply put, vitamin E is the cell's cannon fodder in its interminable battle with free radicals.

The mineral selenium works with vitamin E to protect cardiac and skeletal muscle tissues. Selenium is part of an enzyme that works to protect the interior of the cell, while vitamin E protects the outer portions of the cell.

Vitamin E is a common term applied to the substance tocopherol (pronounced "toe-KOF-er-all"), of which there are at least 8 known variants. The word tocopherol comes from the Greek words *tokos* (childbirth), and *pherein* (to carry, or bear), while the *-ol* ending denotes that it is an alcohol. It was so named after it was discovered that vitamin E would allow female rats, being fed rancid fat, to carry their pups to term. While vitamin E will be guaranteed on a feed label in IU per pound, tocopherol is customarily referred to in milligrams. Fortunately, one milligram of tocopherol is equivalent to one IU of vitamin E activity, a tidy fact that makes the terms interchangeable for all practical purposes.

As with most other nutrients, deficiencies of vitamin E are most evident in young, growing horses. Young horses deprived of vitamin E experience a rapid degeneration of cardiac and skeletal muscles. Noticeable symptoms include exaggerated, uncoordinated movement, especially in the hind limbs, and a "sprawled" stance.

While the NRC has set no minimum requirement for vitamin E, it suggests that all horses should receive at least 50 mg. of tocopherol per kilogram of dry feed, while pregnant and lactating mares, growing foals, and performance horses might do better with 80 mg./kg. of dry diet. Since most forages and grains contain less than 30 mg./kg. of tocopherol (and hay considerably less if it has been rained on), some degree of supplementation would be helpful for most horses.

Pregnant mares need vitamin E to maintain normal reproductive function, and lactating mares need an extra supply to pass on to their foals in their milk. Young, growing horses require extra vitamin E to help with normal muscle development. Performance horses should have additional vitamin E to maintain the integrity of muscles that are constantly bombarded with the harmful oxidative by-products of anaerobic respiration. And, although it has never been conclusively proven that vitamin E improves a stallion's libido, most stallion owners—myself included—would not dare weather a breeding season without it.

If we assume that the non-supplemental portion of a normal diet contains around 30 mgs./kg. of tocopherol, this would leave a deficit of 500 – 600 IU of vitamin E for the average broodmare; 250 - 300 IU per day for a 3 - 4 month-old foal; and 650 – 750 IU per day for a performance horse in heavy training. There is no shortage of vitamin E supplements on the market. Most contain 2,000 IU per ounce, in the form of dl-alpha tocopherol acetate (a stable form of tocopherol). Many include trace amounts of selenium. The manufacturers of these supplements recommend feeding 2,000 IU per day to stallions, broodmares and horses in training, and sales are brisk. Aside from the cost, there is certainly no harm in feeding that much tocopherol to horses and, according to many trainers and farm managers, the benefits far outweigh the costs.

Young horses deprived of vitamin E experience a rapid degeneration of cardiac and skeletal muscles. Noticeable symptoms include exaggerated, uncoordinated movement, especially in the hind limbs, and a "sprawled" stance.

How much vitamin E is too much? More than most people can afford to feed. While vitamin E toxicity has never been observed in horses, the NRC feels the upper safe limit to be 75 IU per kilogram of body weight per day, or 37,500 IU for an 1100 pound horse.

Vitamin K

Vitamin K is required for the normal clotting of blood. Since it is synthesized in adequate quantities by bacteria in the gut, it's not considered to be of dietary significance for the horse. Vitamin K_3, as menadione, is often present in small quantities in vitamin supplements, and especially in preparation for "bleeders" (race horses that bleed through the lungs due to the rupture of pulmonary capillaries), though its efficacy in those preparations remains to be seen. While oral menadione appears to be relatively non-toxic, injectable menadione given for hemorrhage can cause acute kidney failure and death.

Water-Soluble Vitamins

The water-soluble vitamins include thiamin (B_1), riboflavin (B_2), niacin, pantothenic acid, pyridoxine (B_6), folic acid, choline, vitamin B_{12}, ascorbic acid (vitamin C), and biotin.

Thiamin (B_1)

The importance of thiamin (also known as thiamine) was discovered in 1890, on the island of Java, where it was found that the symptoms of beriberi could be reversed by feeding unhusked rice to affected individuals who previously had been subsisting on polished rice. Thiamin was isolated some 30 years later, and was synthesized for the first time in 1936.

The need for thiamin is directly related to the caloric requirements of the horse. In the body thiamin is converted to thiamin pyrophosphate, a compound required for the metabolism of pyruvic acid. Pyruvic acid, in turn, is an essential link in the chain of reactions leading to the utilization of carbohydrates and proteins. If metabolic thiamin is lacking, the horse cannot derive sufficient energy from its diet.

Although some thiamin is synthesized by bacteria in the gut, it does not appear to be enough to meet the thiamin requirement of the horse, since a deficiency can be triggered by feeding a thiamin deficient diet.

Signs of deficiency include nervousness; dull haircoat; loss of appetite; weight loss; lack of coordination in the hind quarters; and slowed or irregular heartbeat. A deficiency can occur from feeding poor quality hay, or by the inges-

A deficiency of thiamin can occur from feeding poor quality hay, or by the ingestion of certain plants known to make thiamin unavailable to the body.

tion of certain plants known to make thiamin unavailable to the body. These plants include horsetail, yellow star thistle, and bracken fern.

The NRC suggests that 3 mg./kg. of dry feed is sufficient for maintenance, growth and reproduction, while 5 mg./kg. may be needed for the performance horse. Common cereal grains contain concentrations of thiamin in the range of 3 – 6 mg./kg.; dried forages even less. Brewers yeast, on the other hand, is an excellent source of thiamin, as it contains 85 – 90 mg./kg. of thiamin. Unfortunately, brewers yeast is fed in such small quantities that it cannot contribute significant amounts of thiamin to the total ration.

While some degree of thiamin supplementation would probably be helpful for all horses, it is especially beneficial for performance horses. Thiamin can help restore the appetites of horses that have gone off their feed, and in many cases it can help alleviate the nervousness of stall-bound horses on high-energy rations.

Thiamin is usually included in small quantities in

vitamin/mineral supplements. There are also a number of thiamin supplements on the market which contain concentrations from 100 to 1000 milligrams per ounce. These supplements are safe for your horses—if not your pocketbook—as the maximum safe limit for thiamin is at least 1000 times the minimum requirement.

Riboflavin (B₂)

Riboflavin is present in a number of enzymes systems involved in converting feed into energy, which makes it essential to every cell in the body. A deficiency of riboflavin has never been produced in the horse, but in the rat it causes retarded growth, hair loss, dermatitis and reddening of the eyes.

Horses synthesize riboflavin in the large intestine, but not quite enough to meet their daily demands. A minimum of 2 mg./kg. of dry diet is required. Good quality hay should contain 5 – 10 mg./kg. of riboflavin, while most grains contain less than 2 mg./kg.

Riboflavin supplementation should not be a concern for most horses, although performance horses on high-calorie diets may utilize their feed more efficiently with a little extra riboflavin. There is really no point in feeding a lot of it, because it cannot be stored in the body to any extent, and whatever is not used is quickly excreted, via the normal pathways.

Niacin

Niacin is the common term applied to two substances—nicotinic acid and nicotinamide—both of which have equal vitamin activity. The name "niacin" was adopted to avoid confusion—or repulsion by association—with the addictive alkaloid, nicotine. The nutritional significance of niacin was discovered in 1938, when it was found to be the nutritional factor lacking in the diets of dogs with "black tongue disease," and in people with pellagra. These conditions are characterized by loss of appetite, muscular weakness, digestive disorders, dermatitis and anemia.

Niacin is a part of two coenzymes that are critical in the metabolism of carbohydrates, fats and amino acids. Some niacin is synthesized by microbes in the gut, from the amino acid tryptophan. Ample amounts can also be found in forages, protein sources and cereal grains, although most of the niacin in grains is bound in unusable forms.

There is no dietary requirement established for niacin, as no one has ever observed a niacin deficient horse. Just the same, niacin often finds its way into vitamin supplements, sometimes in relatively large amounts. Don't ask; I don't know.

Pantothenic Acid

Pantothenic acid, a component of coenzyme A, is involved in energy metabolism. It is also essential for the synthesis of steroids, including cholesterol, and for the production of adrenal hormones. To some degree, it's synthesized in the intestine, but a dietary source is also needed.

No one really knows the dietary requirement for pantothenic acid, since a deficiency has never been observed in the horse, but 15 PPM in the diet is generally considered adequate. Brewers yeast is an excellent source, with over 80 PPM. Good quality hay should contain at least 20 PPM, while cereal grains range from 5 – 10 PPM.

Pyridoxine (B$_6$)

Pyridoxine is another vitamin that is a component of enzyme systems involved in the metabolism of protein, fats and carbo-hydrates. It is also required for the formation of red blood cells. Pyridoxine is the form of vitamin B$_6$ found in plants. It is later converted in the body into pyridoxal and pyridoxamine.

Pyridoxine is synthesized by microflora in the gut, and is found in small amounts in forages, grains, and protein sources. No minimum dietary requirement has been estab-lished for pyridoxine, as no deficiency of this vitamin has ever been observed in the horse. But since it is a component in the systems that turns feed into energy, the need for it increases with the energy demands of the horse. For that reason, it is often added to supplements for performance horses and preg-nant mares.

Folic Acid

It was recently discovered that adding folic acid to the diets of prenatal women would greatly reduce the incidence of cer-tain forms of birth defects. The FDA was so impressed that they immediately issued an order requiring flour manufac-turers to add folic acid to the flour they produced for human consumption. They later bolstered this proclamation by requiring any "enriched" bread or breakfast cereal to provide at least 10% of the minimum requirement of folic acid in each serving.

To find a meaningful correlation with horses may be difficult, however, since one of the richest sources of folic acid—grass—is a common feed for horses and a most uncom-mon one for humans. In fact, most of what a horse eats is richer in folic acid than most of what people eat (except for those of us who enjoy green, leafy vegetables), so the likelihood of a deficiency in horses—especially one leading to birth defects—is slight.

To find a meaningful correlation with horses may be difficult, however, since one of the richest sources of folic acid—grass—is a common feed for horses and a most uncommon one for humans.

Folic acid has a number of functions in the body. It is needed for the formation of red blood cells, the synthesis of methionine, and the formation of nucleic acids.

While it is known that folic acid is synthesized by intestinal bacteria, it is not certain how much of a horse's daily requirements are met by this process. For this reason, the dietary requirement has not been established for the horse. However, since no signs of deficiency have ever been reported, a normal diet is thought to contain sufficient folic acid.

Just the same, folic acid is usually included in vitamin supplements, where it may be of some benefit to pregnant and lactating mares (who always need more of everything), and performance horses, since folic acid is lost in sweat and also because they manufacture more blood than most other horses.

Choline

Choline is a compound that is always included in discussions of water-soluble vitamins, albeit with some hesitancy. Unlike the other B vitamins, choline has no known catalytic role in the body, which is to say that it's not a part of any enzyme, or coenzyme. It is further set apart from other members of the group by the fact that it's synthesized in the liver, rather than in the intestine.

Although it may be different, choline is still vitally important. As a constituent of acetylcholine, it is needed for the transmission of nerve impulses from neuron to neuron. It acts in synergy with methionine as a methyl donor, where it has a role in fat metabolism. Choline is also a structural component of cell membranes.

For all of its many metabolic roles, no one has ever studied the horse's requirements for choline, just as no one has ever produced a choline deficient horse. The abundance of choline in forages and grains can easily make up for any shortfall in metabolic synthesis, making a deficiency highly improbable. Just the same, choline chloride (which is quite inexpensive) is added in liberal amounts to most vitamin supplements.

Vitamin B_{12} (Cobalamin)

Vitamin B_{12} is another vitamin that stands out among the water-soluble vitamins. Containing a single atom of cobalt in its core, it is not produced by any plants, even though plants take cobalt into their tissues. The only natural vitamin B_{12} is produced by microorganisms, many of which are found in the horse's intestines.

Vitamin B_{12} was the last vitamin to be discovered

(1948) and, considering how little of it is needed, it is the most potent. And yet it shows no signs of toxicity in amounts several hundred times what is considered necessary.

Vitamin B_{12} is essential for the production of red blood cells, and for this reason it is almost always included in vitamin supplements (usually in the form of cyanocobalamin) formulated for performance horses. Interestingly, these supplements also contain ample amounts of cobalt—just to cover all the bases, I would imagine.

The organs of the body, primarily in the liver, can store Vitamin B_{12} indefinitely, so horses deprived of cobalt, or horses suffering temporary depletion of intestinal microflora (from parasites or disease) can rely on their stores of B_{12} for weeks or months, if necessary. There is no evidence of a dietary need for vitamin B_{12}, beyond what is synthesized in the gut.

Ascorbic Acid (Vitamin C)

On food labeled for human consumption, ascorbic acid is referred to as "vitamin C"; on feed and supplements labeled for horses it must be guaranteed as "ascorbic acid." The difference arises not from a double standard for horses and humans, but from the fact that horses manufacture ascorbic acid in their livers, from glucose, while humans do not. For us, as well as other primates, ascorbic acid must be present in the diet. For humans, then, ascorbic acid is a vitamin; for horses it is simply a metabolic essential.

Ascorbic acid's most important role in the body is in its capacity as a cofactor in the synthesis of collagen, the most prevalent protein in the animal world. Collagen is, literally, the protein that holds us—and our horses—together. It is a primary constituent of connective tissues, including skin,

Horses manufacture ascorbic acid (vitamin C) in their livers, from glucose, while humans do not. If you buy a supplement and feed it for no other reason than to provide the horse with an extra source of ascorbic acid, you are probably wasting your money.

tendons, bone and cartilage.

Ascorbic acid is added to a whole range of supplements, especially those formulated to help repair damaged cartilage, or in preparations for bleeders. While the fundamental logic of this is evident, in practice it's of little or no value. Why? Because ascorbic acid is very poorly absorbed by horses, probably because it is broken down by microflora before it ever gets to the bloodstream. It takes a dose of 5 grams or more to raise the level of ascorbic acid in the blood, and 20 or more grams per day to be of significant value.

There is no dietary requirement for ascorbic acid in the horse, since there appears to be no significant dietary pathway for its utilization. This being said, there are many supplements on the market today that contain a new, esterified form of ascorbic acid. (Most notably, the patented product, Ester-C™.) You will find it primarily in products designed to help with collagen formation and joint repair and maintenance—namely, products which include glucosamine and chondroitin sulfates. For humans this is a good thing, as tests have shown esterified ascorbic acid to be a very palatable, non-irritating and absorbable form of ascorbic acid. But most of these studies have been conducted either with human volunteers or with a special strain of Japanese rats, both of which—unlike the horse—lack the ability to manufacture ascorbic acid, and therefore have more highly developed systems for optimizing its absorption from dietary sources. In contrast, no one—to my knowledge—has ever shown that esterified ascorbic acid is nutritionally significant to the horse, an animal that stands out among all others in its muted capacity for utilizing it.

Of course, like all issues, this one has a practical side. If the joint repair supplement you are feeding does contain ascorbic acid—in whatever form—it certainly can't hurt. On the other hand, if you buy a supplement and feed it for no other reason than to provide the horse with an extra source of ascorbic acid, you are probably wasting your money.

Biotin

For over a decade, biotin has been at the center of a heated debate involving horsemen, feed manufacturers, various state agriculture officials, the FDA, and of course, the horse. The controversy over biotin is so intense that the FDA has, in the past, quarantined biotin as an "unapproved animal drug." While this may appear to be a cavalier bureaucratic move, the FDA is actually on solid legal footing, since according to the "Federal Food, Drug and Cosmetic Act," a substance is treated as a drug as soon as someone claims it has a drug-like effect, be it biotin or beef broth.

What could possibly be so controversial about a B-complex vitamin? Well, it all began in the late 1970s when a British feed mill proprietor and a veterinarian decided to add 10 – 15 milligrams of biotin per day to the rations of certain horses under his care, to see if it could help the unacceptably poor condition of their hooves. After 5 months of biotin supplementation, the condition of all the affected hooves had, in fact, improved dramatically.

This was big news, and once it got out, the supplement manufacturers were climbing over the top of each other to be the first on the market with a biotin supplement. New companies sprang up overnight. Promotional literature and advertisements making miraculous claims for the effect this vitamin could have on hoof quality soon followed. All the hype immediately hit a vulnerable spot with the horse-keeping public; after all, a horse's hoof is like a person's hair: no matter how good it looks, it can always look better.

Can biotin help a horse with bad feet? In most cases the answer is yes, although the people doing the research are hard-pressed to explain how, or why.

Meanwhile, the FDA was frantically reading and clipping all of these sensational ads and adding them to the dossiers it keeps on each supplement manufacturer. By the definitions set forth in the "Federal Food, Drug, and Cosmetic Act," the manufacturers were making "drug claims," even though most of the ads clearly stated that biotin was a vitamin. Once the FDA had seen enough, it mobilized its army of agents, who began paying friendly visits to the supplement manufacturers. Ads were pulled, literature seized, and products with suggestive names removed from the market. The battle lines were drawn.

The problem for the FDA was (and is) that biotin is a vitamin, and vitamins fall outside of its jurisdiction. As long as the supplement manufacturers do not claim that biotin can do things the FDA is not convinced it does, they are free from bureaucratic entanglements. This was really no problem for the manufacturers, because any copywriter worth her or his salt can lead you to believe that a given substance can do anything, without actually claiming that it has any effect, whatsoever. I know this to be true, because I used to be one of those copywriters.

But the fire of controversy has, for the most part, burned itself out, though certain state agricultural officials still hold a grudge of such enduring dimensions that they steadfastly refuse to believe that supplemental biotin is of any help to the horse, no matter what evidence to the contrary is put in front of them.

All that being said, the question remains—can biotin help a horse with bad feet? In most cases the answer is yes, although the people doing the research are hard-pressed to explain how, or why. Biotin, like several other B-vitamins, is an integral part of a number of enzymes involved in the synthesis of glucose, fats, proteins, and even RNA and DNA. A horse, or a horseman, could not live long without it. Most plants contain small amounts of biotin, though most of it is bound to proteins that inhibit absorption in the gut. Fortunately, biotin is synthesized in the intestine to such an extent that a biotin deficiency has never been described in the horse. Even horses with pathologically bad feet have blood biotin concentrations comparable to those horses with good feet, making it doubtful that weak, crumbly hooves are caused by a simple deficiency of biotin.

Nonetheless, in study after study, horses with poor hooves have responded to treatment with biotin, supplemented in amounts ranging from 10 to 20 milligrams per day. Treatment periods for these various trials have ranged from 5 months to 2 years, and often the hooves of the treated horses return to their original weak, thin-walled condition after supplemental biotin is removed from the diet.

What is going on here? It has been suggested that biotin might help inhibit the premature decay of the horn cells comprising the outer wall of the hoof. This would keep the wall strong and pliable while new horn is laid down in an environment much more conducive to growth. But this does not explain why horses with bad feet have as much biotin in their blood as horses with good feet. There may be other nutrients involved, the need for which might be compensated for by an abundance of biotin. Or it may be related to the single atom of sulfur in the biotin molecule, since sulfur is vitally important to the health of the hoof.

No one knows for certain, but odds are that a horse on good feed that still has bad feet can be helped with supplemental biotin.

Quick Summary of Vitamins

- **Vitamins** are nutrients needed by the body, though they do not fit into the categories of carbohydrates, fats, proteins, or minerals.
- **Vitamin A** is needed for vision, cell differentiation, and the remodeling of bone. It is manufactured in the body from carotenoids. **Vitamin A (as beta carotene)** is abundant in fresh, green forages, but generally lacking in other feeds.
- **Vitamin D_2** is more abundant in dried forages than fresh ones.
- **Vitamin D_3** is manufactured under the skin in the presence of sunlight.
- **Vitamin D** regulates the absorption of calcium and magnesium, and the excretion of phosphorus. A **vitamin D** deficiency manifests itself as a deficiency of these minerals.
- **Vitamin E** is needed for normal muscle development and reproductive function. As an antioxidant, it protect muscles cells from the oxidative by-products of anaerobic respiration.
- Broodmares, growing foals, breeding stallions and performance horses should all receive some supplemental **vitamin E.**
- **Vitamin K** is needed for the normal clotting of blood. Intestinal bacteria synthesize sufficient **vitamin K** for most horses.
- **Thiamin** and **riboflavin** are both necessary for energy metabolism. Supplemental **thiamin** is beneficial to horses on high carbohydrate diets.

continued

Quick Summary of Vitamins *continued*

- A deficiency of **riboflavin** has never been produced in the horse, but horses with high energy demands may be helped by adding **riboflavin** to the diet.

- **Niacin** is part of two enzymes necessary for carbohydrate, fat and protein metabolism. A deficiency has never been observed, or created in the horse.

- **Pantothenic Acid** is a component of an enzyme involved in energy metabolism, synthesis of steroids and adrenal hormones.

- **Folic Acid** is needed for the formation of red blood cells, the synthesis of methionine, and the formation of nucleic acids.

- **Choline** is necessary for the transmission of nerve impulses, and as a methyl donor in fat metabolism.

- **Vitamin B$_{12}$** is essential for the production of red blood cells. It is manufactured in the gut in the presence of cobalt.

- **Ascorbic acid** is manufactured in the horse's liver from the blood sugar, glucose. Its most important function in the body is in the synthesis of the connective protein, collagen.

- Dietary **ascorbic acid** appears to be of little benefit, since it is very poorly absorbed.

- **Biotin** is part of several enzymes involved in the synthesis of glucose, fats, proteins, and nucleic acids.

- **Biotin** has been shown to help horses with poor-quality hooves, though the reason remains elusive.

CHAPTER 10

Exotic Nutrients

1888

"*Of late years a class of traders has sprung up who profess to sell 'patent foods,' or nostrums,* which are to be cast into the manger with the corn. The economy and the marvelous effects of these secret preparations are loudly trumpeted; and from the numbers who now deal in such articles, these persons evidently find many customers.*"

DR. EDWARD MAYHEW, *ILLUSTRATED HORSE MANAGEMENT*, 1888

*I*f you never fed your horse anything other than the nutrients we've discussed up to this point, your horse would probably live a long and healthy life. This is not to say that we have covered every nutrient known. Chromium, silicon, nickel and fluorine—all needed by the horse in very small quantities—are among the other nutrients adequately supplied by natural feeds. Thousands of compounds exist in feed that the body can make use of, and each of these could rightly be called a nutrient.

But there are other nutrients, politically hot nutrients, on the market these days that are racking up millions of dollars in sales each year. If you live in certain states (Texas comes to mind) these nutrients are controlled as strictly as cocaine, and subject to seizure by state authorities.

Often these nutrients are referred to as "nutraceuticals," because they appear to have drug-like effects on the body. But, as an FDA inspector candidly admitted to me a few years ago, so does ice water. And, since I don't believe in substances that are half-drug and half-nutrient—any more than I believe in Minotaurs—I'll stick to the designation of Exotic Nutrients. Besides, it has a nicer ring to it.

The nutrients discussed here—MSM, DMG (dimethylglycine), glucosamine and chondroitin sulfates, and bromelain—all occur naturally, either within the horse's tissues or in natural feedstuffs. All are expensive nutrients administered in small quantities, and all are things the FDA wishes it had never heard of. They are big ticket items in the feed room, and yet horsemen are lined up to buy them. I do not advocate the use of any of these nutrients, but neither do I feel their use to be unwarranted. None has shown any toxic properties when used according to the manufacturer's instructions. It has been my experience that horsemen are among the least gullible people on the planet, and I have no doubt that those of us with good horses and thin pocket-books would not be shelling out money, again and again, to buy things of no value. If you have performance horses, you've probably lost competitions to horses being fed these nutrients. On the other hand, you have probably won against others, who relied on these nutrients at the expense of good protein and sufficient carbohydrates. There are a hundred ways to win any game, but if the basics are forgotten, what remains is a hundred ways to lose.

MSM (Dimethyl Sulfone)

If I had one-tenth of the money paid to the lawyers who have haggled over the rights to this diminutive molecule, I would probably be writing this book from the porch of a cabin on Isla de las Mujeres, in the Gulf of Mexico, rather than my home in the foothills of Colorado.

MSM is a naturally occurring compound. Its use in animal feeds (and human foods) was formerly covered under several fiercely defended patents that have since been over-turned. Its alarming popularity brought the FDA into the fray several years ago, when the agency brought suit against a prominent supplier of MSM in an abortive attempt to have the substance classified as a food additive, rather than a food. Under that classification, it would fall under the FDA's juris-diction, and could be removed from the marketplace at its whim. Much to the FDA's chagrin, it was proven that MSM was, indeed, a natural compound (a food) ubiquitous in the plant and animal kingdoms, and therefore could not be clas-sified as a food additive.

MSM is an acronym for methylsulfonylmethane, also known as dimethyl sulfone. Structurally, it's as elegant as it is simple: a central sulfur atom is straddled between two

methyl (CH_3) groups, and two oxygen atoms. MSM is manufactured from DMSO (dimethyl sulfoxide), a by-product of
paper manufacture. By treating DMSO with hydrogen perox-
ide in a potentially explosive reaction, you get MSM and
water.

Nutritionally, MSM has
two things going for it: like the
amino acid, methionine, and
the vitamin, choline, MSM is a
methyl donor, which makes it
a player in fat and energy
metabolism. Also, MSM is an
excellent source of metaboli-
cally available sulfur, a fact of
no small significance. At present it is believed by most

MSM has been used successfully
(though not in controlled studies) to help, or cure: epiphysitis;
navicular disease; arthritis; pulmonary hemorrhage (bleeders
syndrome); dull hair coat; and
dry, brittle hooves.

authorities that methionine is the body's most important
source of dietary sulfur, but it's wasteful and inefficient for
the body to tear protein apart to free up sulfur.

The importance of sulfur in the body is well known,
though the requirements for it are not. As noted earlier, sulfur is present in the vitamins biotin and thiamin, the amino
acids methionine and cystine, and in chondroitin sulfates.
Sulfur gives shape and structural support to virtually all the
tissues of the body.

MSM is abundant in fresh green forages (but not dried
hay) and in mare's milk. (Curiously, it is also found in coffee,
tea and beer.) That it is a normal constituent of the equine
diet is not in dispute. Neither is the fact that MSM is an excellent source of dietary sulfur. The nagging question is, what
mode of action could MSM have in the body to account for
the broad range of conditions it's reputed to treat? Is it simply
from the free sulfur it provides, or is there something else?

Neither of these questions has ever been adequately answered.

The conditions to which MSM has been applied are legion, and I have no intention of listing them all, but a few of the more important applications deserve mention. MSM has been used successfully (though not in controlled studies) to help, or cure: epiphysitis; navicular disease; arthritis; pulmonary hemorrhage (bleeders syndrome); dull hair coat; and dry, brittle hooves. The reports are both anecdotal accounts from individual horsemen and veterinarians, and research findings from trained investigators.

Is MSM a useful nutrient? Yes, though it's probably not the panacea that so many over-zealous marketing people claim it is. If you feed it, feed it for the sulfur, and a world of good things can come from that, alone.

DMG (Dimethylglycine)

DMG—known to chemists as N, N-dimethylglycine—has been called a vitamin (vitamin B_{15}) by some researchers; pangamic acid by the Russians; a food additive and a drug by the FDA (who has had no luck in getting the courts to follow either line of reasoning); and a food, by those companies who market it.

Whatever you call it, DMG is a natural compound in food and feed, and animal tissues. Its metabolic roles have been well researched, although the resulting physiological implications are still being fleshed out. Probably of most interest to horsemen is the way in which DMG assists in the process of aerobic respiration. It appears to aid in the transport of oxygen

Probably of most interest to horsemen is the way in which DMG assists in the process of aerobic respiration.

across the cell to the mitochondria, small organelles within the cell where energy reactions take place. By making more oxygen available for aerobic respiration, DMG delays the buildup of lactic acid in the muscles, as well as helping to breakdown the lactic acid in muscles and blood. Since lactic acid is a limiting factor in the quality of a performance—and the recovery time following the performance—any nutrient that enhances respiration is potentially beneficial.

DMG has been on the market since the 1970s, and has been used safely by thousands of human and equine athletes.

Chondroitin Sulfates and Glucosamine

Connective tissue, particularly joint cartilage, is composed primarily of three substances: water, collagens (proteins that are the basic building blocks of connective tissues), and proteoglycans, which are long chains of glycosaminoglycans (GAG's) in a protein matrix. Among the GAG's, those most widely distributed throughout the body are chondroitin sulfates.

Chondroitin sulfates are not a natural part of the equine diet. Although they do occur in some plants, they are tightly bound to other compounds that inhibits their digestion. Rather, they are synthesized within the connective tissue by specialized cells called chondrocytes. Dietary chondroitin sulfates are usually purified from bovine trachea, although they can be found in shark cartilage and in the green-lipped mussel, a mollusk harvested off the coast of New Zealand.

The rationale for feeding something to a horse that is not a natural part of its diet is simple: since we ask horses to do things they do not naturally do, then we may need to feed them things they do not naturally eat. No horse left on its own would beat itself up as badly as a race horse. The extra, unnatural stresses put on the joint cartilage can easily break it down at a faster rate than the body can repair it.

Since chondroitin sulfates are such important compounds in the maintenance of joint tissues, it would seem only logical to feed these substances to our horses. Besides adding to the inventory of cartilage repair material, chondroitin sulfates have been shown to stimulate the chondrocytes to produce their own GAG's, and to inhibit the production of enzymes destructive to joint tissues. But, as with anything, we have to ask how well it will be utilized by the body, since we know the body has a natural—and sometimes nagging—tendency to break big things down into small things. Fats are broken down into fatty acids, proteins into amino acids, complex sugars into simple sugars, and so on. How well will the enormous chondroitin sulfate molecule—with a hefty molecular weight of 14,000—fare within the machinations of such an efficient rendering operation?

Studies show that dietary chondroitin sulfates are, in fact, utilized by the body; perhaps with as much as 40 percent efficiency. But that doesn't mean that 40 percent of the molecules are absorbed, intact. Instead, they are probably all broken down into constituent compounds, which later recombine within the joints.

While 40 percent is certainly better than nothing, no one ever passed a math test with such a feeble score. Might there be a better way to go about protecting our horses' joints from the ravages of competition, and Father Time? Why not feed the precursor to chondroitin sulfate, something small and stealthy that can sneak through the digestive machinery relatively unscathed?

Something like glucosamine.

Glucosamine is probably the most important building block of the above mentioned glycosaminoglycans (GAG's). It is found in abundance in the synovial fluid that lubricates the joints, in chondroitin sulfates, and is necessary for the production of collagen. In other words, it's required for the manufacture of practically every compound needed for growth and maintenance of healthy joints.

Perhaps most importantly, chondrocytes—the cells responsible for the manufacture of cartilage (and chondroitin sulfates)—determine how much cartilage they can make by how much glucosamine is available. For most horses most of the time, there is ample glucosamine on hand. But, during periods of stress, the supply may fall far short of demand. Moreover, in certain degenerative joint diseases, the body is actually instructed to slow production of glucosamine, creating an inhibitory bottleneck in the repair supply line. No bricks, no building.

For most horses most of the time, there is ample glucosamine on hand. But, during periods of stress, the supply may fall far short of demand.

Now the big question: are you better off feeding straight glucosamine, or should you feed glucosamine mixed with chondroitin sulfates? The research on the subject is as voluminous as it is ambivalent. For years it was felt that the two, taken together, delivered an irresistible one-two punch that could almost always overwhelm the degenerative influences that can haunt a horse's joints, but recently a consensus is emerging for glucosamine, alone, as the primary progenitor of joint health. It makes sense. After all, why should you feed chondroitin sulfate—a substance that will be largely discarded by the body—when an abundance of it can be readily made with an ample supply of glucosamine?

Whatever your leanings on the issue, there is a profusion of products to choose from, ranging from pure chondroitin to pure glucosamine, and everything in between. Those that contain glucosamine hydrochloride are generally better than those made with glucosamine sulfate, since the former is purer and more stable than the latter.

While supplement shopping, you will also find a number of other ingredients listed with the glucosamine and/or chondroitin. Among them may be zinc, manganese, ascorbic acid (or "vitamin C," if the manufacturer is truly clueless), dl-methionine, and bromelain. Aside from bromelain—which will be discussed below—all of these nutrients come into play in the joint repair process. But are you feeding them in other supplements, already? And if not, are they in meaningful concentrations in the joint supplement you are considering, or are they simply window dressing? (For horses, remember, it takes several grams of ascorbic acid to make even the slightest difference in the serum concentration.) By reviewing the information in the previous chapters, it should be easy for you to determine if you are buying solid nutrition, or marketing hype.

Those products that contain glucosamine hydrochloride are generally better than those made with glucosamine sulfate, since the former is purer and more stable than the latter.

Bromelain

That leaves us with bromelain, something most of us know very little about, yet something we find showing up more and more in horse supplements these days. What is it, and why would we want to feed it to our horses? The name bromelain refers to a class of naturally occurring proteolytic enzymes extracted from the stems of pineapples. Discovered in 1876 and used therapeutically since 1957, bromelain has been around long enough for researchers to get a good feel for its beneficial properties. And there are many benefits; more, in fact, than I could ever find space here to discuss.

Of primary interest to horsemen is bromelain's proven ability to reduce pre- and post-operative pain and inflammation, and pain and inflammation due to acute trauma (such as the pounding a horse's joints take during a competition). Given in significant quantities (more than 5 grams/day) a few days before a competition, then, bromelain could be expected to reduce the severity of any damage a joint suffers, and to aid in the speed at which that joint recovers. This is good news for those of us with competitive horses. Especially since bromelain is easily digested, and has no known side effects.

You will also see bromelain touted as an aid to digestion, and as a vehicle for delivering other beneficial compounds (such as glucosamine) to the cells. True, or false? Well, it does appear to aid human digestion, but how much of that translates to the horse—with a far different digestive apparatus—remains to be seen. As for delivering other beneficial compounds: it has been shown in humans to enhance the activity of antibiotics, though I know of no studies indicating it can likewise enhance the activity of glucosamine (or other nutrients) in horses.

If you find bromelain on the ingredients list of a joint supplement you are considering buying, ask why it's there. And while you're at it, check and see how much you'll be feeding per day. Anything less than the 5000 milligrams (5 grams) may not have the desired effect.

Of primary interest to horsemen is bromelain's proven ability to reduce pre- and post-operative pain and inflammation, and pain and inflammation due to acute trauma.

CHAPTER 11

Closing Considerations:
The Basics

We have spent a good portion of this book discussing minerals and vitamins, because each one is unique and essential to the health of all horses. If any one of the non-energy nutrients were somehow denied a horse, the horse would eventually die. Fortunately, it is practically impossible to deprive a well-fed horse of enough of most of these nutrients to cause it mortal harm, since they are either present in natural feeds, or manufactured in the body. But it's quite easy to deprive a horse of enough energy and protein, and the horseman who does will quickly run into trouble.

Teeth and Parasites

A horse with dental and/or parasite problems will show signs of energy and protein deprivation, no matter how well it is fed. Imagine trying to chew your food if just one molar on one side of your mouth was ¼ inch longer than all the others; all the grinding and chewing of food would be restricted to that tooth, and the one directly below it. Although this usually doesn't happen to people, it is a common occurrence with horses. Horses' teeth are slowly pushed out of their sockets throughout life. This is why the teeth of an older horse appear longer than those of younger horses, even though the teeth stop growing at the age of five. The process of teeth advancing from their bony anchors is not always uniform, and an older horse can often end up with one or more teeth protruding farther than the others. When this happens, the teeth need to be "floated," a dreamy euphemism for "ground, chipped, and broken-off with the Mother of all rasps." They can also be clipped off with nips designed specifically for that purpose. I know you're probably cringing right now, but don't: as painful as this sounds, it actually

A horse that slobbers its food is a prime candidate for having its teeth checked, as is any horse that is a bad keeper.

causes the horse no discomfort beyond that of having its mouth pried open and its tongue held to one side by the vet, since horses do not have nerves in their teeth. A horse that slobbers its food is a prime candidate for having its teeth checked, as is any horse that is a bad keeper.

Internal parasites have been cited as the culprit in most cases of colic, the primary cause of death in horses. But beyond that, parasites—both internal and external—are probably the major cause of unthriftiness in well-fed horses. They range from single-celled organisms, to worms and mites (which are close relatives of spiders), and the one thing they all have in common is that they draw their nourishment from the body of your horse. No area of the country is free of parasites, though as a general rule they are more prevalent in the warmer, southern states. There are a number of good deworming preparations on the market for ridding a horse of parasites. Your veterinarian would be the person to consult for advice on which products to use in your area, and how often they should be used.

Wood, Sand and Sundries

We all know that horses have a tendency to eat things we would rather they didn't—most visibly distressing, perhaps, is the wood in their stalls and paddock fences. Though somewhat more discriminate than cows—in whose stomachs all manner of strange things have been found—horses still manage to ingest their share of unhealthful oddities.

It's our job, of course, to ensure that they eat only those

things that provide them with nourishment. Steel fences and indestructible mangers (hard rubber, impact-resistant plastic, or metal) are a good start. If you do use wood, there are plenty of products on the market—and folk remedies in the common lore—for rendering it unpalatable to your horses.

But what about the earth beneath their feet? In many areas of the United States—notably the dry Southwest—horses have been found to devour life-threatening quantities of sand along with their feed. Unless the problem is corrected, the horse's health will begin to fail and death from sand colic may follow.

If the area where your horse eats is sandy, or gravelly, or simply dry, loose earth, you should take steps to ensure that their feed does not come into contact with the ground. Hard rubber mats—designed to be placed on stall floors—have been used successfully for this purpose, as have concrete pads. It's best to place the feed in a tub or a feeder on the mat, to minimize the amount of "goodies" that fall onto it, as these may, after a time, end up in the sand beside the mat.

Some horses, unfortunately, will eat sand or gravel out of sheer boredom. For these horses, it's a good idea to feed a fiber supplement, especially if you detect sand in the feces. Fiber (as psyllium, primarily) absorbs water in the intestine, and becomes about as slippery as axle grease on an August afternoon. Then—if the problem is not too severe—the normal contractions of the intestine will, in due course, return the sand to Terra Firma, where it belongs. Feed pure psyllium at the rate of 4 ounces per day for 5 days, every month. If you have trouble getting it to stick to the grain, use oil or molasses, but **not** water, since water will make the psyllium expand, leaving a gooey, unpalatable mess for your poor horse to eat.

Feeding Tips

Throughout this book I have stressed *what* to feed a horse, figuring that most of us already know *how* to feed one. However, not all things are obvious, especially for those new to horse care, and a couple of tricks and tips could save you a lot of aggravation.

Feeding Powders

I've never had any trouble feeding powders and small granules since I use a sweet feed with enough molasses that most things stick to it. For those of you who feed whole oats (or some other similarly un-sticky feed) you should try adding a little corn oil. To keep from having a greasy, wadded mess of oil and oats, try putting the oil in a pump bottle, then adding oil to the oats where the powders are to be placed. The powders will adhere, be easy to mix in with the rest of the feed, and your horse will thank you for the few extra calories.

Wintertime Feeding

It's a simple fact of physics that it takes more energy to keep anything warm, once the ambient temperature begins to drop. This means that as the mercury plummets, a horse will need more feed to maintain its 100 degree body temperature. Since body warmth is very high on a warm-blooded animal's priority list, a horse will burn it's own tissues to avoid freezing.

To keep that from happening, you should feed extra hay during cold weather. A general rule of thumb is to feed 10% more hay for each 10 degrees the temperature drops below freezing. (You may think that oats would be better, but in fact the digestion of hay creates more warmth.)

A general rule of thumb is to feed 10% more hay for each 10 degrees the temperature drops below freezing.

Feeding Horses That Bolt Their Food

Lots of horse have atrocious table manners, especially if they are competing with others for a given amount of food. They'll scoop in giant mouthfuls of grain, swallow them without much thought to chewing, then repeat the process. At best it's wasteful, since mastication is a rather important first step in digestion, and unchewed food has a tendency to pass right through the system and end up in the manure pile. At worst, it can lead to choking and colic. To protect your piggish horses—and your feed budget—from their thoughtless excesses, try putting rocks (too big to be appetizing, please) in the feeder. Your horse may not enjoy having to finesse the grain into its belly, but he'll be better off for it.

Forages

I have spoken at length about forages throughout this book, and have given average analyses for a number of the nutrients they each contain. More consideration has been paid to dried hays, rather than pastures, because most horses depend on hays for roughage. The hays used in the examples—alfalfa, bromegrass, orchardgrass and timothy—are a good representation of the hays commonly fed to horses. Alfalfa is a legume, which means that it fixes atmospheric nitrogen in nodules in its roots. In essence, legumes possess the ability to fertilize themselves. Other legumes used for forage include red clover and birdsfoot trefoil, both of which are similar in composition to alfalfa. All of the hays used as examples also make excellent pastures. As pastures, they are all high in nutrients, though their moisture content may prevent a horse from consuming enough to meet its energy needs. So even with green, lush pasture, supplemental feed should be a consideration. Other pasture grasses, such as Bermudagrass or Bahiagrass, grown primarily in the southern states, are less digestible than northern grasses. If poor hay and pasture is the norm in your part of the world, beet pulp fed with an additional protein source (such as soybean meal) makes a good forage.

Most horses will eat between 1% and 2% of their body weight in dry forages every day. For those of us who rely on baled hay, this means that we have to procure two to four tons of hay each year for every horse we own, a fact that underscores the importance of finding good hay. The way in which hay is put up can have at least as great an effect on its nutrient value as the soil on which the hay is grown. Hay that was rained on will have far less nutritional value than hay that was baled without rain. Overly dry hay will likewise be less nutritious than hay that was baled with adequate moisture, and the dust it puts off may cause respiratory problems, such as heaves, in some horses. When examining hay, look for a rich, green color inside the bale, a pliability to the leaves, and an absence of

Most horses will eat between 1% and 2% of their body weight in dry forages every day.

mold and dust. Good hay put up badly is worse than poor hay put up right.

When examining hay, look for a rich, green color inside the bale, a pliability to the leaves, and an absence of mold and dust.

If you are feeding hay that you're not familiar with, it's advisable to have it tested for digestible energy, crude protein, calcium and phosphorus, and any other nutrient you have concerns about. Even though hay may look good, it might be deficient in nutrients.

A word of caution about grass clippings: it is really not a good idea to feed your horse grass clippings from your lawn, unless you spread them out over a large area where the horse will have to spend hours picking them up. Although it is certainly a natural feed for horses, it is too much of a good thing. Its rapid fermentation in the gut can induce a life-threatening case of gas colic.

Grains, Fats, and Extra Protein

Cereal grains are energy feeds. Pound for pound, they supply about half-again as much energy as hay. Of the three grains discussed throughout this book, corn is the highest in digestible energy, followed by barley, and then oats. All three grains generally have protein values between 7.5% and 12% (with corn at the low end), making them comparable in protein to average hay.

Oats, corn and barley, either alone or in combination, make excellent feed for horses. They are the feed of first resort when more energy is needed in the diet. Knowing the caloric needs of the different classes of the horse is of primary importance, since everything that goes on within the horse requires energy.

Soybean meal and flaxseed meal are good sources of essential fatty acids, particularly the Omega-3 fatty acids.

As noted earlier, fat is also an excellent source of energy. Fat should be a consideration for any horse with high caloric demands, such as race horses, where a source of more concentrated energy is needed to cut down on the sheer bulk of feed. Vegetable oils, particularly corn oil, are better sources of fat than animal fats; they are more palatable and are less likely to become rancid. Soybean meal and flaxseed meal are good sources of essential fatty acids, particularly the Omega-3 and -6 fatty acids.

Some form of supplemental protein is beneficial to most horses, and critically important to others, such as growing horses and lactating mares. Additional lysine in the diet can improve the overall protein quality. Besides the sources already mentioned (soybean, cottonseed and linseed meals), peanut meal, sunflower meal and dehydrated brewer's grains (malt pellets) are also good protein sources and, with the exception of brewer's grains, all are high in lysine. Dried skim milk is a good source of animal protein; it is palatable to the horse and it is also high in lysine compared to most vegetable proteins.

Eight Basics of a Successful Feeding Program

1. Good teeth
2. Absence of parasites
3. Good hay or pasture
4. Ample sources of energy
5. Sufficient sources of good protein

And, lest we forget:
6. A clean, sand-free feeding area
7. Salt (preferably iodized), free choice
8. Good water, free choice

If all of the above are provided for your horse, your chances of having feed-related problems will be minimal. But if one or more of these eight items is overlooked, well . . . . No, I don't need to say it.

ACKNOWLEDGMENTS

I wish, first and foremost, to thank my wife, LaVonne, for her help in making *Beyond the Hay Days* what it is. Her keen insight, natural sense of design, and razor-sharp editing skills have made this a far better book than it would otherwise have been.

Lifelong thanks to my mother, who decided long ago that I could heal from anything my horses could do to me, so she never discouraged me from keeping company with them; and my father, a gentleman, a horseman, and a self-proclaimed "dirty gut fighter," who taught me that defiance is a virtue; nutrition is a science, and its application is an art.

Every reader will be grateful for the many fine illustrations by Sara Tuttle and I owe her my special thanks. I would also like to thank Dr. Donald Mackey for making several insightful suggestions and corrections. Dr. Mackey has been in practice longer than I have been around to bang up horses for him to treat, and several generations of horses have led better lives for that fact. Over the years, Dr. Mackey has taught me a number of techniques that have helped me to better care for my horses. My favorite was a hands-on tutorial on how close not to stand to a horse when administering a tranquilizing dart.

Additional thanks go Dr. Earl E. Ammerman, whose knowledge of minerals will forever astound me; Dr. Larry Mackey, the only veterinarian I know of with a Master's degree in nutrition, whose left-handed techniques lead to an occasional wreck because of my right-handed bungling; Joe and Lee Hatch, who together produce the best horse feeds found anywhere; Jim Olson, nutritionist, who took me under his wing when I was young and naïve; Mary Jane Seale, for research help; and finally, Cherry Hill and Richard Klimesh—*Beyond The Hay Days* has been greatly enriched by their suggestions.

Of course, any mistakes, omissions, understatements, overstatements, lapses of good judgment or grammatical snafus are entirely my own.

APPENDIX A
GUIDE TO SUPPLEMENTAL FEEDING

We have covered over 30 nutrients in the preceding pages, and I have offered suggestions for when it would be most appropriate to include these nutrients in the rations of the various classes of horses. But unless you have a far more tenacious memory than I, you will probably find yourself flipping back and forth between pages to keep it all straight in your mind. This makes for dog-eared books and frustrated readers. So, to keep this book—and your patience—intact, I have put together the following 2-page chart as a guide to supplemental feeding, the operative word here being "guide." It is **not** designed to cover every horse, in every situation. No chart could ever do that. It **is** an easy reference to use when considering the applicability of feeds and supplements to your feeding program.

It is not within the chart's parameters to address the needs of horses suffering from disease, injury or other pathological conditions, such as heavy parasite loads, or nutrient imbalances caused by improper feeding or peculiar soil conditions. For instance, when it is suggested that biotin supplementation is probably not critical for most horses, it should not be construed to mean that biotin is not an effective means to improve the condition of poor-quality hooves. By the same token, an anemic horse may well be helped by the addition of vitamin B_{12} to the diet, even though the chart shows that supplementation is of little or no value. Conversely, if you live in an area with high iodine concentrations in the soil, you do not need to supplement iodine, no matter what the chart indicates.

I have not included carbohydrates here, since they are the basis of all natural feeds. Nor have I included the *Exotic Nutrients*; the use of these nutrients is purely a matter of choice by the individual horseman in consideration of each individual horse.

And remember: even though we horsemen are an independent lot who like to work things out on our own, it never hurts to seek the advise of a good nutritionist or veterinarian, or a reputable feed company when formulating rations.

APPENDIX A
GUIDE TO SUPPLEMENTAL FEEDING

	Maintenance Horse or Early Pregnancy	Late Pregnancy	Lactating Mare	Growing Horse	Performance Horse	Breeding Stallion
Protein	★	❖	◆	◆	❖	❖
Fat	★	★	★	★	❖	★
MINERALS						
Calcium	✪	❖	❖	❖	❖	✪
Phosphorus	✪	❖	❖	❖	❖	✪
Magnesium*	★	★	★	★	❖	★
Sulfur	★	★	★	★	★	★
Potassium	✪	✪	✪	✪	◆	✪
Salt	◆	◆	◆	◆	◆	◆
Cobalt	★	★	★	★	★	★
Copper	★	❖	❖	◆	❖	❖
Iodine	◆	◆	◆	◆	◆	◆
Iron	★	★	★	★	★	★
Manganese	✪	❖	❖	◆	◆	❖
Zinc	◆	◆	◆	◆	◆	◆
Selenium	✪	✪	✪	✪	✪	✪

* NOTE: Magnesium should be supplemented if the diet contains excessive calcium.

◆ Should definitely supplement, except under extraordinary conditions.
❖ Should probably supplement.
★ May be supplemented, but probably not critical.
✪ Supplementation depends on amount present in feeds.
○ Should not supplement, or supplementation is of little or no value.

APPENDIX A
GUIDE TO SUPPLEMENTAL FEEDING

VITAMINS	Maintenance Horse or Early Pregnancy	Late Pregnancy	Lactating Mare	Growing Horse	Performance Horse	Breeding Stallion
Vitamin A	❖	❖	❖	❖	❖	❖
Vitamin D	★	❖	❖	❖	★	★
Vitamin E	★	◆	◆	◆	◆	◆
Vitamin K	○	○	○	○	○	○
Thiamin (B$_1$)	★	❖	❖	❖	◆	❖
Riboflavin (B$_2$)	★	★	★	★	❖	★
Niacin	★	★	★	★	★	★
Pantothenic Acid	★	★	★	★	❖	★
Pyridoxine (B$_6$)	★	❖	❖	★	❖	★
Folic Acid	★	★	★	★	❖	★
Choline	★	★	★	★	★	★
Vitamin B$_{12}$	✪	✪	○	○	○	○
Ascorbic Acid	○	○	○	○	○	○
Biotin	★	★	★	★	❖	★

◆   Should definitely supplement, except under extraordinary conditions.
❖   Should probably supplement.
★   May be supplemented, but probably not critical.
✪   Supplementation depends on amount present in feeds.
○   Should not supplement, or supplementation is of little or no value.

APPENDIX B
HELPFUL FORMULAS & CONVERSION FACTORS

In preparing the tables for this book I used several different mathematical conversions to put the information into forms that were readily understandable. Many of them were intuitive, others were not. For those who do not work with these units on a daily basis, I will give a few formulas that should enable anyone to translate a feed label into easier terms, and thereby formulate their own rations.

Feed labels are a marriage of metric and avoirdupois units, which is a mixed blessing. People who are familiar with the metric system find it logical and easy to use. Every unit is a power of ten above or below another unit. Units of volume are equivalent to units of liquid measure, such that a cubic centimeter (cc) is the same volume as a milliliter (ml), which makes 1000 cc's equivalent to a liter. Furthermore, the metric system is based on the specific gravity of water at standard temperature and pressure, which means that one gram of water occupies one cc (or one milliliter) of space, and one liter (1000 cc's) of water weighs one kilogram. (By contrast, how many people know how many cubic inches are in one gallon of water?)

This is all well and good, except that most of us were brought up thinking in ounces, pounds, feet, inches, pints, quarts, and gallons. Whenever we see grams, the brain asks for ounces. Unfortunately, ounces just do not work when dealing with small quantities, such as the amount of copper in a pound of sweet feed. It is much easier to say "18.5 milligrams" than "1/1532nd of an ounce."

Like it or not, the metric system is a fact of life when it comes to horse feeds, and the horseman who takes the time to become familiar with it will be miles (or kilometers) ahead of the neighbor down the road, who doesn't.

Metric Conversion Factors
One Pound = 16 ounces
One ounce = 28.35 grams
One pound = 453.6 grams
One pound = 453,600 milligrams
One pound = 0.45 kilograms
One gram = 1000 milligrams
One kilogram = 1000 grams
One kilogram = 2.2 pounds

Percent to Milligrams per Day

Percentages are used extensively in feed labeling. Protein, fat, fiber, calcium, phosphorus, magnesium and salt are always guaranteed in percentages, and often other minerals will be, too.

QUESTION
If you are feeding 4 pounds of a sweet feed that guarantees 0.012% zinc, how many milligrams of zinc are you feeding per day?

SOLUTION
1. **Convert pounds of feed to milligrams:**
    4 lbs. x 453,600 mg./lb. = 1,814,400 milligrams
    (see chart on page 148 for conversion factor)

2. **Convert percentage of zinc to actual value:**
    (divide by 100, or move the decimal point 2 places to the left)
    0.012% ÷ 100 = .00012

3. **Multiply total milligrams (#1) by the number from #2:**
    1,814,400 mg. x .00012 = 217.728 mg. of zinc in
    4 pounds of feed.

YOUR TURN

1. **Convert pounds of feed to milligrams:**
    _____ lbs. x 453,600 mg./lb. = _____ mg.

2. **Convert percentage of nutrient to actual value:**
    _____ % ÷ 100 = _____

3. **Multiply total milligrams (#1) by the number from #2:**
    _____ mg. x _____ = _____ mg. in ____ lbs.

Percent to Grams per Day

It works just the same with minerals like calcium, except that we use grams instead of milligrams.

QUESTION

How many grams of calcium are in 5 pounds of feed with a 0.6% calcium content?

SOLUTION

1. **Convert pounds of feed to grams:**
   5 lbs. x 453.6 g./lb. = 2268 grams
   (see chart on page 148 for conversion factor)

2. **Convert percentage to actual value:**
   (divide by 100, or move the decimal point 2 places to the left)
   0.6% ÷ 100 = .006

3. **Multiply total grams (#1) by the number from #2:**
   2268 g. x .006 = 13.608 grams of calcium in 5 lbs. of feed

---

YOUR TURN

1. **Convert pounds of feed to grams:**
   ____ lbs. x 453.6 g./lb. = _____ g.

2. **Convert percentage of nutrient to actual value:**
   _____ % ÷ 100 = _____

3. **Multiply total grams (#1) by the number from #2:**
   _____ g. x _____ = _____ grams in ____ lbs.

PPM to Milligrams per Day

Trace minerals, such as zinc, copper, iron, etc., should be guaranteed as PPM, or "parts per million".

QUESTION

If you are feeding your horse two ounces per day of a supplement that guarantees 8500 PPM of iron, how many milligrams of iron is the horse getting?

SOLUTION

1. **Convert ounces of supplement to grams:**
   2 ounces x 28.35 g./oz. = 56.7 grams
   (see chart on page 148 for conversion factor)

2. **Convert grams (#1) to milligrams:**
   (multiply by 1000, or move the decimal point 3 places to the right)
   56.7 grams x 1000 = 56,700 milligrams

3. **Convert PPM to actual value:**
   (divide by 1,000,000 or move the decimal point 6 places to the left)
   8500 PPM ÷ 1,000,000 = .008500 or .0085

4. **Multiply total milligrams (#2) by the number from #3:**
   56,700 mg. x .0085 = 481.95 milligrams of iron in 2 ounces of supplement

YOUR TURN

1. **Convert ounces of supplement to grams:**
   ____ *ounces x 28.35 g./oz. =* ____ *grams*

2. **Convert grams (#1) to milligrams:**
   _____ *grams x 1000 =* _____ *milligrams*

3. **Convert PPM to actual value:**
   _____ *PPM ÷ 1,000,000 =* _____

4. **Multiply total milligrams (#2) by the number from #3:**
   _____ *mg. x* _____ *=* _____ *milligrams*

Total Protein in a Ration

QUESTION

Let's say you are feeding 14 pounds of hay that is 12.5% protein and 6 pounds of supplemental sweet feed that is 16% protein. What is the protein percentage of the entire ration?

SOLUTION

1. **Find the protein factor for each feed:**
   14 lbs. hay x 12.5% protein = 175
   6 lbs. sweet feed x 16% protein = 96

2. **Add the protein factors and the total pounds:**
   protein factors: 175 + 96 = 271
   14 lbs. + 6 lbs. = 20 lbs.

3. **Divide total protein factor by total pounds:**
   271 ÷ 20 lbs. = 13.55% protein in the entire ration.

QUESTION

How many grams of protein are in the ration listed above?

SOLUTION

1. **Convert total pounds to grams:**
   20 lbs. x 453.6 g./lb. = 9072 grams

2. **Convert total percentage to actual value:**
   (divide by 100, or move the decimal point 2 places to the left)
   13.55% ÷ 100 = .1355

3. **Multiply total grams (#1) by the number from #2:**
   9072 g. x .1355 = 1229.3 grams of protein in the entire ration.

SUGGESTED READING

Nutrient Requirements of Horses, Fifth Revised Edition, 1989.
National Research Council; National Academy Press.
> *Packed with information about nutrients and nutrition, including feed tables giving the nutrient composition of practically everything you would ever want to feed your horse.*

Horse Nutrition, A Practical Guide. Harold F. Hintz, Ph.D.; Prentice Hall Press, 1988.
> *A little dated, but still my favorite. Dr. Hintz does an excellent job of handling a difficult subject with an easy conversational style.*

Veterinary Notes for Horse Owners, 17th Edition. Captain M. Horace Hayes, F.R.C.V.S.; Prentice Hall Press, 1987.
> *Fairly technical, but offers good advice for feed and feeding related problems. The 18th Edition (published by Simon & Schuster) is now available.*

The Horse, 2nd Edition. J. Warren Evans, Anthony Borton, Harold Hintz, L. Dale Van Vleck; W. H. Freedman & Company, 1990.
> *The title pretty much says it all. This book includes discussions of feeds and nutrients, feed related problems, and tables listing the nutrient compositions of most common feeds. The 3rd Edition is currently available.*

I also recommend these titles by Cherry Hill
for practical feeding advice and overall horse management
(available from www.horsekeeping.com):

Horsekeeping on a Small Acreage
Stablekeeping
Horse Health Care
The Formative Years

LIST OF TABLES, CHARTS & SUMMARIES

INDEX

italics indicate table, chart or list

ABOUT THE AUTHOR

Rex A. Ewing grew up in northeastern Colorado's Platte valley, where he spent most of his time looking after the family's herds of Charolais cattle and Thoroughbred horses. He learned early about the importance of proper feeding since, in addition to the purebred stock, the Ewing Ranch operated an experimental feedlot for horses, cattle and sheep, where his father, John, tested the efficacy of different feeds and additives.

Following college, Rex returned to life on the ranch, managing the horse operation and assisting his father in the family's horse nutrition business. When John Ewing died in 1990, Rex became president and CEO of the John Ewing Company, a world-renowned producer of horse nutrition products. Combining his years of common-sense experience with the scientific particulars of horse nutrition, he formulated a number successful products, wrote regularly for horse publications, and talked to thousands of horse owners about their nutrition related problems.

After leaving the business in 1997, Rex wrote the first edition of *Beyond the Hay Days*. Since then, he has maintained his contacts and followed the industry closely. Today he lives with his wife, LaVonne, in the mountains of Northern Colorado.

Rex A. Ewing's other books include:
Logs, Wind and Sun: Handcraft Your Own Log Home...
    Then Power it With Nature (PixyJack Press, 2002)
Power With Nature: Solar and Wind Energy Demystified
    (PixyJack Press, 2003)

Logs, Wind and Sun
Handcraft your own log home...then power it with nature.
by Rex A. Ewing and LaVonne Ewing

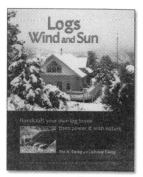

An inspiring, hands-on guide to self-sufficiency that takes you through every step of handcrafting your own log home and then bringing it to life with power from the wind and sun. Drawing on their own experiences, and those of others in the Colorado Rockies, the authors show you—simply and enjoyably—just how attainable your dream of off-grid, log home living can be.

Power With Nature
Solar and Wind Energy Demystified
by Rex A. Ewing

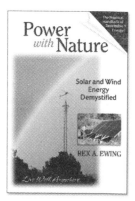

This practical handbook of renewable energy is packed with hands-on information about generating your own electricity from the sun and wind, from a man who lives what he writes about. Written in easy-to-understand language, and filled with dozens of photos and illustrations. The comprehensive appendix includes worksheets, tables, solar maps, and a detailed resource section.

To order autographed copies, please visit our website or write to us at the address listed below.

PIXYJACK PRESS LLC

PO Box 149 • Masonville, CO 80541
www.pixyjackpress.com